save
buk

11 & 12
TOURISM
STUDIES

PNG UPPER SECONDARY

John Ngunts Imbal

T0363586

OXFORD

OXFORD
UNIVERSITY PRESS

Oxford University Press is a department of the University of Oxford.
It furthers the University's objective of excellence in research,
scholarship, and education by publishing worldwide. Oxford is a registered
trademark of Oxford University Press in the UK and in certain other
countries.

Published in Australia by
Oxford University Press
253 Normanby Road, South Melbourne, Victoria 3205, Australia

© Oxford University Press 2013

The moral rights of the author have been asserted

First published 2013
Reprinted 2014, 2021

ISBN 978 0 19 552475 8

Reproduction and communication for educational purposes
The Australian *Copyright Act 1968* (the Act) allows a maximum of one chapter
or 10% of the pages of this work, whichever is the greater, to be reproduced
and/or communicated by any educational institution for its educational purposes
provided that the educational institution (or the body that administers it) has
given a remuneration notice to Copyright Agency Limited (CAL) under the Act.

For details of the CAL licence for educational institutions contact:

Copyright Agency Limited
Level 15, 233 Castlereagh Street
Sydney NSW 2000
Telephone: (02) 9394 7600
Facsimile: (02) 9394 7601
Email: info@copyright.com.au

Typeset by diacriTech, Chennai, India
Printed in China by Golden Cup Printing Co. Ltd

*Links to third party websites are provided by Oxford in good faith and for information only.
Oxford disclaims any responsibility for the materials contained in any third party website
referenced in this work.*

Contents

Introduction

Year 11 and 12 Tourism Studies covers eight Units, each of which is illustrated by four to eight Topics or sub-topics. These Units and sub-topics provide the material to support teaching and learning at the Upper Secondary School Curriculum in Papua New Guinea. This is to enable successful completion of Tourism Studies units 11.1 to 12.4 – Learning Outcomes.

The Learning Outcomes for Tourism Studies identify the knowledge, skills, attitudes and values all students should achieve and demonstrate at the end of Grade 12. The Syllabus (page 5) lists them as follows:

1. Demonstrate an understanding of tourism at the local, national, regional and international level.
2. Describe and explain the growth of local, national, regional and global tourism.
3. Identify the role of tourism in the economic growth of a country.
4. Demonstrate an understanding of the impact of tourism at individual, local, national, regional and global levels.
5. Demonstrate an understanding of the principles of good management and customer service.
6. Communicate tourism information in a variety of ways and settings.

The table below sets out the eight Units and their titles, weeks of study and correspondence to the Learning Outcomes in Upper Secondary Tourism Studies Syllabus page 5 for Grades 11 and 12 in Papua New Guinea.

Unit	Unit title	Weeks	Matches outcomes numbers
11.1	Introduction to the Tourism Industry	10	1, 2, 4
11.2	Tourism in Papua New Guinea	10	1, 2, 3, 4
11.3	Our Neighbours and Tourism	10	1, 2, 4, 6
11.4	Tourism Information	10	1, 3, 4, 6
12.1	Global Tourism	10	1, 2, 4, 6
12.2	Tourism as a Business	10	3, 4, 5, 6
12.3	Customer Service	10	1, 5, 6
12.4	Option: Tour Guiding	10	5, 6

It is assumed that teachers will read the Syllabus and use this book as their main resource book. But teachers should supplement the information presented here by using other resources. For example, the statistics presented were the latest available at the time of going to print, but teachers should access more up-to-date data from the Internet and other sources; they should also use the Internet and other sources of information to introduce a variety of relevant case studies.

Acknowledgments

This book has been produced with the help of several people whom I want to thank here: my colleagues, namely, Vanessa Uiari for her contributions to Unit 11.1 Topic 3, Elizabeth Goodyear for her contributions to Unit 11.1 Topic 4 and Nathaline Murki for her contributions to Unit 11.1 Topic 5. My sincere gratitude to Robert Banasi of Divine Word University Community Information Centre for his work on the original manuscript design and layout, and to Albert Serre Pou. Finally, I would like to acknowledge Tobias Gena and the Curriculum Development and Assessment Division of the Papua New Guinea Department of Education for their support.

John Ngunts Imbal

Copyright acknowledgments

The author and the publisher wish to thank and acknowledge the following copyright holders for reproduction of their material.

Reprinted from *Annals of Tourism Research*, vol. 17, no. 3, 1990, pp. 432–48, Seoho Um & John L. Crompton, 'Attitude Determinants in Tourism Destination Choice', with permission from Elsevier, p. 72. Extracts from *Tourism Management*, 2000, John Wiley & Sons, Inc. – this material is reproduced with permission of John Wiley & Sons, Inc., pp. 73, 122 (top). Diagram from *Marketing for Hospitality and Tourism* (3rd edn), Pearson Higher Education USA, 2003 – reproduced by permission, p. 86 (top). Diagrams from *Tourism Management*, by Neil Leiper, 2005, RMIT Press, Melbourne – reproduced by permission of RMIT Press, pp. 97, 99. Richard Jones, colour section p. 1 (top, centre and bottom left), colour section p. 2 (top), colour section p. 3 (top and centre). All other photographs supplied by the author.

Every effort has been made to trace the original source of copyright material contained in this book. The publisher will be pleased to hear from copyright holders to rectify any errors or omissions.

To Ngunts Gilma and Elisabeth Taim Plang
Yutupela givim mi olgeta samting na ino askim wanpela samting long mi.
Dap Kerma elep pil ngonda.

Unit 11.1 Introduction to the Tourism Industry
Topic 1: Tourism

In line with the Syllabus (page 8) the first Unit focuses on the social and environmental implications of tourism as an activity and as an industry. It looks at the positive and negative impacts of tourism – environmental, social, economic and cultural – and at sustainable tourism, especially at the community level. Students are expected to:

- Demonstrate an understanding of tourism at the local, national, regional and international levels.
- Describe and explain the growth of local, national, regional and global tourism.
- Demonstrate an understanding of the impact of tourism at individual, local, national, regional and global levels.

Topic 1 introduces the concept of tourism and defines the meaning of tourism. Students will consider:

- The historical development of tourism.
- The definition of tourism.
- Tourism industry sectors.

Introduction – historical development of tourism

Travel is central to human existence. In one sense, the **concept** of tourism goes back to earliest times, when all human beings were nomads and travel was the typical way of life. **Nomadic travel** can be regarded as a form of tourism because it was probably undertaken for cultural and **recreational** purposes, as well as for reasons of survival.

Historically, in the **pre-industrial era** in Europe, travel for pleasure was mostly limited to the wealthy and privileged. Some of the earliest European **travellers** were the **explorers**. Among those who visited our part of the world were Jorge de Meneses, William Dampier, Philip Carteret and Louis-Antoine de Bougainville. Those explorers combined business (exploring or colonising distant lands) with pleasure (**sightseeing**).

What links today's tourism phenomenon with the pre-industrial era is the **Grand Tour**. The wealthy elites of Europe (especially in the 18th century) would take a round-trip **tour** of western Europe, usually passing through France, Italy, Switzerland, Germany and the Low Countries. Their motive was to explore and enjoy the capital cities, politics, art, **culture** and society of these countries.

The Industrial Revolution of the mid-18th to mid-19th century saw an increase in travel by Europe's middle class, as the **economic** boom provided more employment and income-earning opportunities. England's Thomas Cook and Company emerged as a pioneer in the development of the modern **tourism industry**.

The huge growth in tourist numbers in the 20th century, particularly since the advent of the jet age in the 1950s, is the result of travel by people from all **social** classes who can afford it and from a larger number of countries, and the availability of faster, more affordable means of transport. What used to be an activity limited to the English could now be imitated by other Europeans, then by Americans and later by people from other parts of the world.

Accounts of early tourism in Melanesia by Douglas (1996) show that of some 76 papers delivered at meetings of the Royal Queensland Geographical Society between 1885 and 1897, one-third were travelogues on New Guinea or Melanesia. One of the early promoters of travel and sightseeing to Melanesia was the Burns Philp trading company, which advertised a 'New Guinea **excursion** trip' in the *Sydney Morning Herald* on 16 February 1884. The five-week sailing trip would leave Thursday Island on 10 March and take in Darnley Island, Yale Island, Hall Sound, Port Moresby, Hule, Kerepune and Aroma before returning to Thursday Island via Port Moresby. A short stay was planned for each stop. In the numerous tourist itineraries that followed, passengers were accommodated on board and when they came ashore at each stop they were entertained by missionaries, government agents, traders and planters, with occasional visits to nearby **indigenous** villages. Competing with each other to attract this tourist **traffic** were two famous **hotels**, the Papuan Hotel and the Port Moresby Hotel.

The first official **guest house** in PNG was reportedly built at a cost of £756 14s 11d (approximately K2300) by John Douglas, special commissioner of the protectorate of British New Guinea. It was leased to a Jean De Raeve of Townsville who operated it as the Granville **Boarding House** until 1887, when he fell into debt, abandoned the boarding house and returned to Australia. (Today, there is a hotel in Port Moresby called the Granville Hotel, but it is unknown whether it is related to the original boarding house.) Other adventurous types include John Goldie, a travelling **botanist** in the mid-1870s, and the famous Russian traveller, explorer and **anthropologist** Nicolai Miklouho Maclay, who stayed for some time with the Raicoast people in Madang.

The arrival of the first missionaries and the setting up of colonial administration led to further inbound tourist activity. The first Roman Catholic missionary activity in New Guinea began in 1847, when French Marist missionaries established a station on Woodlark Island. In 1886 the Reverend Johann Flierl established the first Lutheran base, at Simbang in the Finschhafen area of Morobe Province. Missionaries would stay for some time at these main stations and then return to their **outstations**. Because of this, a small house with rooms, just like a guest house, was built to accommodate travelling missionaries.

During the colonial era, such as during William MacGregor's reign as administrator of British New Guinea (1884–1906), an administrative **system** was established that linked Port Moresby with the rest of the **colony**, which was divided into four divisions. Each division had a resident magistrate, who would ensure that any **visiting officials** had a house in which to stay temporarily. Although not built specifically for the purposes of tourism as we understand it today, these residences were similar in concept to a guest house and this official travel was a form of tourism.

The stories and activities of our **ancestors** tell us about their involvement in tourism. One example is the kula trade in the Milne Bay Province. As shown in Malinowski's map opposite, the Kula Ring followed a circular route around Milne Bay. By custom the necklaces (called bagi or soulava) were considered **masculine** and travelled clockwise, whereas the arm-shells (called mwali) were considered **feminine** and travelled anticlockwise. Travel from one island to another was temporary; there was exchange between the trading partners, as between the chiefs of distant islands; no doubt the bands of trading partners were welcomed in the spirit of Melanesian **hospitality** with an exchange of gifts. This meets the definition of **domestic tourism**: it involved domestic travellers; there was temporary travel; travellers were welcomed and services provided as in hospitality; and the travel resulted in an exchange that benefited both visitors and hosts. This shows that tourism has long existed in our cultures, and that we can draw upon this tradition to improve tourism in PNG.

In more modern terms, formal tourism began in PNG with parliament's passing of the *Tourism Promotion Authority Act* in 1993, which set the foundation for government policy and support.

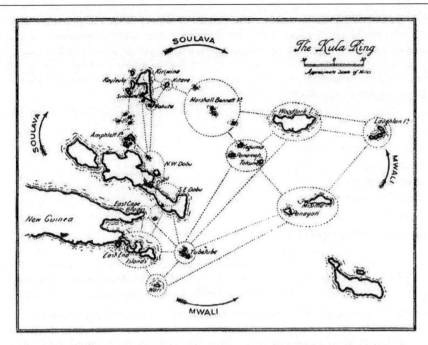

Malinowski's map of the Kula Ring, also known as the Kula Exchange (source: Malinowski 1932)

Defining tourism

The *Oxford Advanced Learner's Dictionary* defines tourism as 'the **business** activity connected with providing **accommodation**, services and **entertainment** for people who are visiting a place for pleasure'. Tourism involves temporary travel by a person to somewhere outside their usual **place of residence** for at least one night, with the person taking part in tourism activities. Because tourism is a business, it is important to collect and analyse data and produce reliable statistical reports.

The three primary subjects of tourism studies are the person travelling (the tourist), temporary travel, and involvement in tourism activities.

The three main elements of tourism: tourist, temporary travel and tourism activity

If there is no travel, there is no tourism. The human element in tourism is important because the person who travels and spends money creates employment through their **demand** for activities such as diving, snorkelling, trekking and mountain climbing and for services such as guest house accommodation. By temporary travel, we mean that the person will return to their usual place of residence or origin after they have been to another place or destination (indicated by the arrows in the previous illustration).

A more comprehensive definition and study of tourism involves other essential components or elements, such as:

- A tourist-generating region.
- Transportation.
- **Transit regions**.
- Destination tourism activities.
- Destination tourism products.

A **tourist-generating region** is where the tourist plans and begins his or her trip. It is usually their place of residence (e.g. Europe is the tourist-generating region for a family planning to travel from France to PNG for diving). **Transportation** is important because it enables people to travel from the generating region to a destination region. A **tourist destination region** is where tourists spend their money and time, enjoying that destination's tourism activities or products.

Sometimes there are stops during the journey to allow travellers to connect to onward transportation. During these stops travellers can buy food or souvenirs, take photographs and so on, all of which activities form part of tourism's contribution to the **economy** and create employment in those areas. These transit regions are important because they serve the needs of travellers while transiting through to their destination or when returning to their **place of origin**. For instance, someone travelling from Alotau to attend a conference in Madang has to transit through Port Moresby. While waiting at Jackson's Airport the person buys a newspaper to read, a cup of hot coffee to drink and a pack of sandwiches to eat, before boarding the next connecting flight to Madang. Money spent by such travellers is one of the economic benefits of tourism to the economy.

Tambua Sands Beach Resort is in Fiji's Coral Coast region.
Guests stay in traditional bures (bungalows).

In-flight snacks served by Air Niugini

Cruise ship Pacific Pearl *is operated by P&O (established in England as the Peninsular and Oriental Steam Navigation Company in the early 19th century).*

Reliable transportation is an essential part of tourism infrastructure in any country.

Why do you think traditional handicrafts are a popular attraction
in Papua New Guinea and many other Pacific nations?

Other important aspects are known as the 'Five *As*' of tourism:

- Attractions.
- Accessibility.
- Accommodation.
- Amenities.
- Activities.

Attractions are places, events or activities that motivate tourists to travel, such as the annual migration of wild animals, the fireworks display of an erupting volcano or typical PNG village life. **Accessibility** requires safe and reliable transportation, as well as access to basic infrastructure and services such as **communication**, health, banking and postal systems. **Accommodation** is a basic need, with accommodation types ranging from home-stays and guest houses in some rural areas, to modern **lodges**, hotels and **self-contained apartments** in urban areas. **Amenities** are basic services and facilities that enhance comfort and enjoyment for tourists and other travellers. They include public toilets, fast food restaurants and takeaways, retail shops and **visitor information centres**.

In addition, businesses providing tourist goods and services, the government of the host area, the **host community** and publicists are all important partners in the promotion and growth of tourism at any destination. Tourism businesses are necessary for providing profitable services and facilities to satisfy **visitors'** needs. The host government is responsible for ensuring proper regulation, **safety** and **security** of visitors and for providing basic municipal infrastructure. Publicists have responsibility for **marketing** and promoting the area as a desirable tourist destination, while the host community primarily owns the natural and cultural tourism **resources** that are found in the area, and shares these amongst its own members and with visitors.

The tourist industry can also be categorised into **sectors**, as shown in the seven-sector analysis in the table below. Such categorisation cannot be precise as boundaries between sectors are often blurred or overlap (such as a **travel agent** who also develops **travel packages** and conducts tours).

Tourism sector	Description
The marketing specialist sector	Comprises travel agents, **tour wholesalers** and promotional agencies; usually based in tourist-generating regions.
The carrier sector	Comprises public transport specialists such as airlines, buses, taxis, railway and shipping lines.
The accommodations sector	Comprises **lodgings** such as guest houses and hotels and related services (such as food and drink) for the travelling public; usually based in tourist destinations.
The attractions sector	Comprises organisations aiming to provide tourists with **leisure** experiences of any kind, for example, parks, entertainment centres, sporting and cultural activities; based mainly in transit regions and destination regions.
The **tour operator** sector	Main purpose is to assemble pre-packaged arrangements for tourists; present in all three regions.

Tourism sector	Description
The coordinating sector	Includes units within government departments of tourism and transport that try to coordinate the operations or strategic development of any other sectors of this industry, e.g. PNGTPA (PNG Tourism Promotion Authority) and IATA (International Air Transport Association).
The miscellaneous sector	A convenient catch-all category for other services and activities, such as souvenir and duty-free shops; may be present in all regions.

Sectors in a tourism industry (source: Leiper 1995). NB tourists are not obliged to use the services of the tourism industry. For example, a tourist might choose to use their own car and stay with friends.

For tourism to work effectively and to prosper, the different elements, components and sectors need to be linked, working together and supporting each other. The tourism industry depends on this network of different **stakeholders** to provide for the satisfaction of visitors as well as meeting the needs of the stakeholders themselves.

Unit 11.1 Activity 1: Tourism

1. Provide an example of each of the following:
   a. Involvement in tourism by your ancestors.
   b. A three-concept model of defining tourism.
   c. A multi-concept model of defining tourism.

2. Describe the role of the following tourism stakeholders:
   a. Local businesses.
   b. Host government.
   c. Host community.
   d. Publicists.
   e. Visitors/tourists.

3. Identify the tourism sector(s) of the following:
   a. Global Travel Centre, a small travel agent in Madang, advertises a one-week holiday to Alotau and nearby islands.
   b. PNGTPA produces new sets of standards for the accommodation sector in PNG.
   c. Kokopo Tours arranges to pick up German tourists from Tokua Airport.
   d. A departing tourist buys a traditional Engan sand painting near Kagamuga Airport.

4. Describe and give an example of the 'Five As' of tourism:
   a. Attractions.
   b. Accessibility.
   c. Accommodation.
   d. Amenities.
   e. Activities.

Unit 11.1 Introduction to the Tourism Industry

Topic 2: Tourists

Having defined the concept of tourism in the previous Topic, we continue our introduction to tourism by considering what we mean by the term 'tourist'. Who are tourists? What are their origins and purpose? Where do they stay and what are their needs and expectations? These are some of the questions addressed in Topic 2 (in line with the Syllabus, page 9).

Defining a tourist

Simply put, a tourist is someone who travels temporarily to another destination to satisfy their leisure needs. Leisure needs are what someone does in their free time, for example, snorkelling, buying **artefacts** at the market or watching a village cultural performance.

The Papua New Guinea Tourism Promotion Authority (PNGTPA) is the national body responsible for fostering the development of tourism in PNG in order to maximise the economic benefits of the industry to PNG, whilst minimising any disruptions to society, culture and the **environment**. For the purpose of producing statistical reports, the PNGTPA gives the following definitions:

- Visitor – a person who travels to a country other than that in which they usually reside, or who travels within their own country but outside their usual environment, for a period not exceeding 12 months, and whose main purpose of visit is not to take up work paid from within the place visited.

- Tourist – a visitor for at least one night whose main purpose of visit falls into one of the following three groups:
  - Leisure and **holiday**.
  - Business and professional.
  - Other purposes.

- **Business traveller** – an employee or other individual who make trips or visits in the course of their paid work, including attending meetings, **incentive** travel, conferences and exhibitions (MICE).

- **VFR** – a person travelling to a destination in order to visit friends or relatives.

- Holiday traveller – a person travelling to a destination for the purpose of a holiday or **vacation**.

These definitions are similar to those used by regional and international organisations such as the South Pacific Tourism Organisation (SPTO) and the United Nations World Tourism Organization (UNWTO). 'Traveller' is a term used generally to mean someone who travels; the person may or may not be motivated by tourism interests. Some countries' statistical reports include 'excursionists' or 'day trippers' – visitors staying for less than 24 hours, including passengers on cruise ships. These terms are sometimes used interchangeably; for instance 'visitor' is sometimes used very broadly to refer to all types of traveller. The UNWTO, the worldwide umbrella organisation in the area of tourism, which serves as a global forum for tourism policy issues and as a practical source of tourism know-how, provides the following classification of tourism concepts, applicable in any country:

- Domestic tourism – tourism by residents within their own country, such as Western Highlanders travelling down to the coast of Madang to do some sightseeing.
- **Inbound tourism** – tourism by non-residents visiting from a different country, such as Americans travelling into PNG to climb Mt Wilhelm (the highest mountain in PNG).
- **Outbound tourism** – tourism by residents travelling outside their own country, such as mothers from East New Britain travelling down to Cairns to do some shopping.
- **Internal tourism** – tourism within a country by both residents and non-residents, such as expatriates and residents from other PNG centres travelling to Port Moresby for the annual Hiri Moale Festival.
- **National tourism** – tourism by people both within and outside their own country, combining domestic and outbound tourism.

Type of tourist	Demand characteristics
Allocentric	Wants adventurous, individual exploration.
Charter	Searches for relaxation and good times in a new but familiar environment.
Diversionary	Escaping the boredom and routine of everyday life; enjoys therapy (healing) through alienation or isolation.
Drifter	Seeks exotic and strange environments.
Elite	Visits unusual places, using pre-arranged native facilities.
Existential	Leaves the world of everyday life and practicality to escape to an 'elective centre' for spiritual sustenance.
Experiential	Looking for meaning in the lives of others; enjoys authenticity or what is original.
Experimental	On a quest for alternative lifestyles; wants to be involved in the authentic lives of others.
Explorer	Arranges own trip and tries to get off the beaten track; wants to interact with hosts.
Incipient mass	Travel as individuals or small groups; seek combination of amenities and authenticity.
Individual mass tourist	Makes travel arrangements to popular destinations through a third party (e.g. travel agency).
Mass	Middle-class income, similar to organised mass tourist.
Mid-centric	Likes individual travel to areas with facilities and a growing reputation.

Organised mass tourist	Usually travels in a group on a packaged or **guided tour**; seeks the familiar.
Offbeat	Avoids crowded places.
Psychocentric	Takes organised, packaged holidays to popular destinations.
Recreational	Travels for entertainment and relaxation to restore their physical and mental powers.
Unusual	Makes occasional side trips to explore isolated areas, or undertakes risky activities.

Types of tourists (source: Murphy 1985)

Statistics on international tourism are easy to gather because of the forms that travellers must complete at airports and seaports in every country. It is more difficult to gather information about domestic tourism, so developing countries often underestimate the contribution of domestic tourism to regional areas. Of course, international tourism also brings in foreign earnings to boost the domestic economy.

For marketing purposes and to better satisfy the needs of tourists, further classification of types of tourists can be made. The table above lists the types of tourists, and their demand characteristics, that are discussed in some literature. Other, more common, names include 'soft-adventure tourist' and 'hard-adventure tourist'. Soft-adventure tourists enjoy easy, low-stress activities such as walks, sightseeing and snorkelling. Hard-adventure tourists prefer more active pursuits such as mountain climbing, hiking and trekking.

Pleasure vacations can also be categorised according to the tourist's motivation and need. Motivation is what causes someone to act, whereas need is a state of felt deprivation. A potential tourist initially feels a need or desire to take a vacation for pleasure; he or she then finds other reasons to go on a pleasure vacation, particularly if the desired activities cannot be done at home.

John L. Crompton documented seven socio-psychological motives and two cultural motives influencing choice of destination for pleasure vacations, as shown in the table on the following page. Socio-psychological motives are the social and mental factors that influence travel decisions and choices, whereas cultural motives emphasise destination traits that influence travel decisions. The latter reflect 'pull factors' that attract tourists to a particular destination, while the former reflect 'push factors' that cause people to wish to travel away from home.

	Travel motive	Explanation
Socio-psychological	Escape	Wanting to escape from a perceived mundane environment; a break from routine.
	Exploration and evaluation of self	Time to re-evaluate or discover something about oneself, and refine or modify one's self-image.
	Relaxation	Achieving mental relaxation, even if physically exhausting.
	Prestige	Improvement to self-image as having travelled, 'been there and done that'.
	Regression	Opportunity to do something different and to be different, undertaking activities which one wouldn't normally do at home.
	Enhancement of kinship relationships	Opportunity to meet and strengthen ties with family members and relatives.
	Social interaction	Allows interaction and exchange with other people and cultures.
Cultural	Novelty	Chance to face new challenges and try new activities and experiences, rather than simply hearing or reading about them.
	Education	Wanting to learn, become more experienced and more knowledgeable as a result of travel.

Motivations to travel for pleasure (source: Crompton 1979)

Different **market segments** or sectors of the tourism industry try to attract particular categories of visitors, such as divers, mountain climbers, trekkers, birdwatchers, nature enthusiasts, conservationists, researchers, photographers, writers, film-makers, students, families or honeymooners. Different establishments tailor their services and facilities to suit the specific needs of their **clientele**. The result is fewer guest complaints and better value for money.

PNG representatives at the ITB (International Tourism Bourse) in Berlin, Germany. The PNG Tourism Promotion Authority and industry members attend this significant event in order to promote and sell Destination PNG.

Unit 11.1 Activity 2: Tourists

1. Give the corresponding tourist term(s) for these descriptions:

    a. An expatriate is visiting PNG for less than 12 months.

    b. A Malaysian is in Port Moresby to attend a meeting.

    c. An Australian visits her cousins in Rabaul.

    d. A Dutch couple spends two days relaxing on the white sand beach of Tugutugu Guest House on Karkar Island.

2. Match the terms with their corresponding descriptions:

1. International tourism	**A.** Arranges their own trip and tries to get off the beaten track; wants to interact with locals.
2. Domestic tourism	**B.** Wants to experience new things in a new and different environment, rather than simply hearing or reading about these things.
3. Explorer	**C.** Inbound tourism plus outbound tourism.
4. Organised mass tourist	**D.** Achieving mental relaxation, even if physically exhausting.
5. Mid-centric	**E.** A tourist travelling within their own country.
6. Psychocentric	**F.** Likes to travel in a group, to familiar places with guiding services provided.
7. Relaxation	**G.** Likes to travel to places with facilities and growing reputation.
8. Novelty	**H.** Takes organised packaged holidays to popular destinations.

Unit 11.1 Introduction to the Tourism Industry
Topic 3: Sustainable tourism

The term 'sustainable' means using natural products and energy in a way that does not harm the environment. It also refers to an activity that can be sustained for a long time. Both shades of meaning are relevant to tourism. Having considered what we mean by the terms tourist and tourism, Topic 3 examines what can be done to sustain tourism and what we can learn from past experiences.

Identifying forms of sustainable tourism

Sustainable tourism is a shortened form of the phrase 'sustainable development of tourism'. It implies efforts to prolong the benefits of tourism for all parties and stakeholders, while minimising the negative consequences of tourism, and caring for the future.

In short, sustainable tourism aims to meet the needs of the present generation, without compromising the ability of future generations to meet their own needs. Sustainable tourism development tries to balance the economic, social and **aesthetic** needs of the host community or destination with the needs of tourists and other stakeholders, while maintaining cultural and environmental integrity.

The diagram below depicts a stakeholder–outcome **model** of sustainable tourism. It explains the many benefits that can flow from sustainable tourism – aesthetic, economic, social, cultural and environmental – and the different stakeholders involved: government and non-government organisations, businesses, publicists, visitors and the host community.

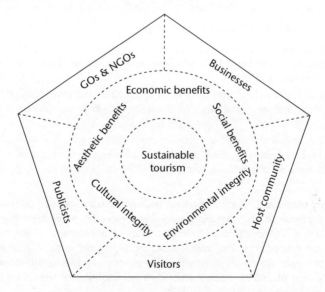

A stakeholder–outcome model of sustainable tourism

- Government organisations are responsible for planning, resourcing and regulating the industry; ensuring the safety and protection of hosts and visitors; and providing **public goods and services** to facilitate tourism.
- Non-government organisations depend on resources and funding from individuals and organisations. They work with other agencies to use their capability and technical know-how to provide skills training and basic services that host government organisations are unable to provide. Businesses bring the host community and visitors together for profit. They provide commercial services that visitors need such as accommodation, transportation and leisure activities.
- The host community is custodian of the cultural and other resources that attract visitors. It uses these resources to benefit its own members and visitors, and is responsible for preserving the resources for future generations.
- Visitors make tourism viable. If they have a good time in the destination there will be positive outcomes such as income for host communities and continued integrity of cultural and environmental resources.
- Publicists comprise the mass media, individuals and organisations who market and promote tourism, including those who carry out awareness-raising and education. Their role is important in getting the right message to all other stakeholders, thus encouraging positive action. They provide information and education so that realistic goals can be met. For example, tourism and hospitality management students from Divine Word University visit nearby villages in Madang to raise awareness of the advantages and disadvantages of **cultural tourism**; this helps communities to prepare themselves so they have realistic expectations of cultural tourism.

It is not realistic to expect that there will be a balance in the outcomes of sustainable tourism or that all stakeholders will benefit equally. Rather, it is important to ensure equitable participation and to achieve the aspirations of sustainable tourism in developing the tourism industry.

According to the UNWTO, sustainable tourism should:

- Make optimal use of environmental resources that constitute a key element in tourism development, maintaining essential **ecological** processes and helping to conserve natural heritage and biodiversity.
- Respect the sociocultural authenticity of host communities, conserve their built and living cultural heritage and traditional values, and contribute to inter-cultural understanding and tolerance.
- Ensure viable, long-term economic operations, providing socio-economic benefits to all stakeholders that are fairly distributed, including stable employment and income-earning opportunities and social services to host communities, and contributing to poverty alleviation.

The UNWTO and other renowned international bodies have recommended principles and practices for sustainable tourism that are contained in some of the publications listed in the table below. These guidelines and management practices are applicable to all forms of tourism in all types of destinations, including mass tourism and the various niche tourism segments. Sustainability principles refer to the environmental, economic, and sociocultural aspects of tourism development, and a suitable balance must be established between these three dimensions to guarantee long-term sustainability.

Organisation	Year	Publication title
UNEP, UNWTO	2005	*Making Tourism More Sustainable: A Guide for Policy Makers*
WTO	2004	*Indicators of Sustainable Development for Tourism Destinations: A Guidebook*
ICLEI	2003	*Tourism and Local Agenda 21: The Role of Local Authorities in Sustainable Tourism*
WTO	2003	*Recommendations to Governments for Supporting and/or Establishing National Certification Systems for Sustainable Tourism*
UNESCO	1999	*Tourism and Environmental Protection. Seventh Session, 19–30 April 1999*
UNWTO	1998	*Sustainable Tourism Development: A Guide for Local Planners*
WTTC, WTO, Earth Council	1995	*Agenda 21 for the Travel and Tourism Industry: Towards Environmentally Sustainable Development*

Publications recommending principles for sustainable tourism (source: Dinica 2009)

There may be other specific sustainable practice industry guidelines for destination authorities, accommodation facilities, recreational parks, etc. Today many countries have developed forms of sustainable tourism that adopt some of the mentioned principles and practices and those produced by organisations listed in the table above. Some examples of practices in sustainable tourism by organisations in PNG are:

Organisation	Sustainable tourism practice	Comment
Ecotourism Melanesia, Port Moresby	'Ecotourism Melanesia offers a wide range of fully resourced soft-adventure experiences that take you into rural areas of Papua New Guinea and bring you face to face with our culturally diverse peoples and unique natural history. And rest assured that we practise responsible tourism and all our tours benefit local communities.'	There is direct contact between visitors and rural host communities so that rural people benefit from tourism; this helps to sustain tourism activities. The organisation's assurance that it conducts responsible tourism will minimise negative impacts on natural and cultural resources.

Napatana Lodge, Milne Bay	'Napatana Lodge specialises in eco-tourism and interacts closely with local communities and environmental groups to encourage the participation of the local villagers. We have an advisory service to help you to plan your trip, either using local transport or charters. We have up to the minute information on all that is happening in the province. Even if you do not stay with us, do drop in for a cup of coffee and we can help you decide what is best for you.'	The lodge uses local resources and involves local communities so they benefit from tourism. It shows concern in trying to help visitors plan and enjoy their trips in the province.
PNG Divers Association	'The Environmental & Safety Fee has been established for two primary purposes; to ensure the continued availability of a hyperbaric recompression facility in Papua New Guinea, help fund operating costs, training programs and to treat Papua New Guinean divers, and to sustain and expand the capacity of the PNG Divers Association to participate in a range of programs and activities in support of ensuring implementation of the Environmental Code of Ethics, and the protection and management of Papua New Guinea's unique marine bio-diversity.'	The organisation collects a fee from the user, which is reinvested in dive resources, protection and management that will sustain quality dive experiences in PNG.
Melanesian Foundation through Melanesian Tourist Services, Madang	'On Feb 14 we visited Boisa aboard the Kalibobo Spirit delivering building and educational material. Our electrician completed the electrification of the solar lighting to 2 classrooms and 2 teachers' houses and delivered 20 new school desks to the delight of the Boisa people. This project is now complete! The Chigier Family who donated US$10,000 should be very satisfied that all their funds, including an additional PGK20,000 from the MTS Foundation was used to equip this remote school on Boisa Island.'	The organisation uses a part of its profits and contributions from its clients and friends to bring services to remote communities in a way that ensures remote communities also share in the benefits of tourism, so that tourism becomes a sustainable activity.

| Kumul Lodge, Enga | 'The Lodge is a locally owned and staffed venture under advice by naturalised tourism experts and overseas environmental protection organisations. It is a rural development project by the people and for the people to better and improve their rural lifestyle. Our aim is to give you the holiday of your lifetime through a small comfortable set up yet with moderate tariffs and a high level of personalised service. We would like you to be in direct contact with nature and the people instead of viewing this from a bus only. Almost all of our vegetables and fruits are getting organically grown on our own vegetable/fruit plantations which are village society projects.' | The organisation works with experts in this field, NGOs and host communities to improve tourism in the area. It is greatly concerned about both the environment and the well-being of guests and hosts alike, so that tourism becomes a sustainable activity in the area. |
| Mahonia Na Dari through Walindi Plantation Resort, West New Britain | 'Mahonia Na Dari's vision is to protect this unique marine environment through raising awareness and educating future generations about what they have and how it functions. This is achieved most effectively through a series of semi structured 10 weeks, 1 day courses attended by selected students from the secondary schools in the area. This Marine Environmental Education Programme (MEEP) has been running now for over 10 years. The learning is focused around integrated resource management and interrelated ecosystems supported by the fundamentals of marine **ecology** and biology. The students also learn new skills; how to snorkel, take comprehensive field notes, lead and participate in discussions and present information in interesting and stimulating ways.' | This organisation uses expert skills and knowledge to impart valuable tourism resource information to community members including students, who will be future decision-makers. This can ensure that tourism resources are protected and properly managed so that their use for tourism purposes can be sustainable. |

Sustainable tourism practice by PNG organisations

Note that some initiatives mentioned above impose additional costs upon organisations, but the initiatives have real benefits for various stakeholders, including for the tourism resources. When most of these needs are satisfied in some way, sustainable tourism development is usually the result.

The table below explains some categories of sustainable tourism. These are all the result of good intentions and aspirations, but when not properly managed they can lead to disastrous consequences and negative tensions. For example, uncontrolled and excessive visitation to ecologically sensitive sites can disturb the feeding and mating habits of wild animals, causing them to be extraordinarily aggressive.

Tourism activity	Explanation
Alternative tourism	Forms of tourism that set out to be consistent with natural, social, and community values, and that allow both hosts and guests to enjoy positive and worthwhile interaction and shared experiences.
	Considers conservation of the environment and the sustenance and well-being of local people.
	Usually small-scale; developed and owned by local people.
	Attracts fewer tourists but with specific interests, to admire, study and enjoy local scenery.
	Can be found in more remote and undisturbed locations.
Community-based tourism	Occurs when decisions about tourism activity and development are driven by the host community.
	Usually involves some form of cultural exchange where tourists meet with local communities and witness aspects of their lifestyle.
	Successful and sustainable if the community hosts tourists on its own terms with the aim of protecting itself from outside influences.
	Communities take pride in the display of their cultural assets such as archaeological ruins, historic sites and traditional crafts production.
	Serves as a means for communities to decide collectively on their needs for development, conservation, self-sustenance, exchange between tourist and host, and improvement in quality of life.
Village tourism	Involves tourists visiting, and staying in or near, a village and experiencing village life.
	Tourists become part of the village for the period of their stay, immersing themselves in daily village activities.
	Opportunity for tourists to learn and assist in community development. However, the influx of tourists can influence local culture, so this has to be managed.
Cultural tourism	Recorded cultural tourism in PNG began with the first Western Highlands Agricultural Show, held in 1961.
	Regarded as a force for cultural preservation.
	Defined as the absorption by tourists of both **contemporary** and past urban and rural lifestyles of a society, observed through phenomena such as handicrafts, languages, traditions, art and music, paintings and carvings, history, work and technology, architecture, religion, educational system, bilas (traditional costume), and leisure activities that reflect the lifestyle of any particular community at a particular time.

	Involves education for visitors, promotes sensitivity towards cultural environment, provides direct benefits to host communities, helps in preservation of culture and becomes an integral part of tourist experience.
Ecotourism	Responsible travel to natural areas, which conserves the environment and improves the well-being of local people.
	Provides effective economic incentives for conserving and enhancing biological and cultural diversity and helps protect the natural and cultural heritage of communities.
	Can be an effective vehicle for empowering local communities around the world to fight against poverty and to achieve sustainable development.
	Promotes greater understanding and appreciation for nature, local society and culture.

Forms of sustainable tourism

Sustainable development of tourism is important if we want to enjoy the benefits of tourism now and in the future. The question of sustainability must be looked at from different perspectives, and as far as possible we must ensure a balance in benefits, with a focus on implementation.

The Tupira Surf Club in Madang promotes sustainable tourism by involving the local community in its management plan and investing a portion of the income in community development.

Final-year tourism and hospitality management students of Divine Word University conducting sustainable culture tourism awareness at Bilbil village in Madang. This is an example of the role of publicists in providing information and education to stakeholders for positive action, so that realistic goals are met.

Unit 11.1 Activity 3A: Sustainable tourism – short-answer questions

1. What are the three main benefits of sustainable tourism?
2. Give an example of how sustainable tourism can lead to:
   a. Economic benefits.
   b. Social benefits.
   c. Aesthetic benefits.
   d. Cultural integrity.
   e. Environmental integrity.
3. Give an example to show how sustainable tourism benefits:
   a. Governments (government organisations).
   b. Non-government organisations.
   c. Businesses.
   d. Host communities.
   e. Visitors.
   f. Publicists.

Unit 11.1 Activity 3B: Sustainable tourism – essay

Write a short essay describing an example of a sustainable form of tourism, based on your own experience or observation. Present it to the class for discussion.

Unit 11.1 Activity 3C: Sustainable tourism – field report

Visit a nearby tourism establishment or project site and draw up a short checklist of what makes the project sustainable or not. Present a field report on your findings to the class.

Unit 11.1 Introduction to the Tourism Industry
Topic 4: Tourism within the local community

In line with the Syllabus page 9, Topic 4 considers the role and effects of tourism within the local community: lobby groups, economic diversification, facilities, business creation and the preservation of the environment and culture.

Describing tourism at the community level

Community tourism is about development in a community context. It takes into account economic, social and environmental well-being. Because tourism relies on places and people, it cannot exist outside a community. Thus tourism and communities coexist and must be viewed simultaneously – any change to one will affect the other. For this reason, tourism is one of the most important community development tools, particularly in marginal communities such as indigenous, remote and rural communities.

Tourism has always had a close connection with communities because the local people act as hosts for the tourists; they also act as guides on tours and are the experts on their surrounding environment and cultures. This interaction has changed slightly as the market shifts from a community (village) perspective to a more national perspective. In some instances, community interaction has become a 15-minute photo opportunity rather than an opportunity for real learning and interaction – a cultural experience.

Due to increased consumer education and awareness and more **sophisticated customer** demands, conservationists and tourism lobby groups are supporting new forms of tourism that respond to growing concern at the environmental damage attributed to traditional tourism. Such groups are seeking ways to mitigate these negative environmental impacts. There is a push for new forms of tourism that meet the increasing desire to preserve the natural environment, through visiting so-called 'wilderness' and virgin territory where nature can be experienced by 'sensitive' new tourists.

Community tourism will have both positive and negative consequences. Although visitors may bring economic benefits, those wishing to experience host cultures will bring with them their own cultures, norms and beliefs, which over time will intertwine with those of their hosts. The community will also have to give up certain privileges if community tourism is to be encouraged. Examples include lifting access restrictions on places such as burial sites and fishing, hunting and gardening areas; putting up with traffic congestion; and even losing some personal privacy due to the constant presence of larg numbers of visitors. Locals can become frustrated by being bombarded by inquisitive outsiders and by having to use their limited resources to support the demands of those visitors. There are also concerns about controlling visitor numbers in order to maintain environmental quality.

Community tourism targets those visitors who are particularly interested in communal life and traditional forms of community organisation. Communities can cater to this interest by offering village stays, tours and immersion in village cultures and activities. Communities need to be well organised to take advantage of this type of development. They must meet health, **hygiene** and safety requirements – proper sewerage and water systems, **signage**, clear tracks and basic medical supply (aid posts and first-aid facilities); maintain law and order; be courteous to guests; provide comfortable accommodation; ensure supplies of dry and frozen goods and consumables such as batteries; and possess knowledge and skills in providing guest service, comfort and security.

The diagram below shows a model of ensuring sustainability and quality in community tourism. It identifies six stakeholders who influence, and are influenced by, community tourism: government, NGOs, businesses, host community, publicists and visitors. Community tourism, if well planned and organised, can provide sociocultural, economic and environmental benefits to all these stakeholders. All of them must participate in and benefit from community tourism if its activities are to be sustained and its quality is to be maintained.

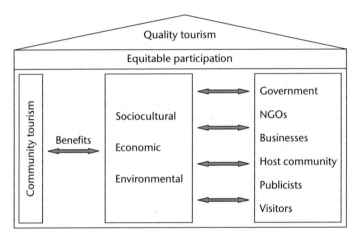

A model of ensuring quality and sustainable community tourism

The host government provides policies, regulations, safety, security and necessary infrastructure. NGOs (non-government organisations) should possess the capability and technical know-how to provide communities with skills training and basic services that formal or elected governments are unable to provide. To do this, NGOs need access to financial and other resources.

Businesses take advantage of opportunities to provide services at a profit. They sometimes need support infrastructure to be in place in order to deliver **quality service** to visitors.

Publicists are the various media, individuals and organisations that market and promote community tourism, including those that carry out awareness-raising and education.

The host community shares its resources with its own members and with visitors; it is also responsible for the present and future image of the community.

Visitors make community tourism viable; it is important that their interests are catered for but also that they are receptive and sensitive to the concerns of the host community.

All these stakeholders must build strong **networking** relationships amongst themselves and must be committed to the cause of ensuring quality and sustainability in community tourism activities so that the benefits can reach all parties. As part of networking, below is a list of tourism organisations in PNG which offer help to communities in planning and organising themselves for better community tourism.

Papua New Guinea Tourism Promotion Authority Pacific MMI Building, Level 5 PO Box 1291 Port Moresby, NCD Tel 320 0211, Fax 320 0223 Email info@pngtourism.org.pg Website www.tpa.papuanewguinea.travel	Madang Visitors and Cultural Bureau PO Box 1071 Madang, MP Tel 422 3302, Fax 422 3540 Email info@tourismmadang.com Website www.tourismmadang.com
East New Britain Tourism Bureau PO Box 385 Rabaul, ENBP Tel 982 8657, Fax 982 8697 Email enbtourism@global.net.pg or enbpa@global.net.au Website www.eastnewbritain.gov.pg/ tourism.htm	New Ireland Tourism Bureau Corner Coronation Drive and Tanga Street PO Box 544 Kavieng, NIP Tel 984 2441, Fax 984 2254 Email nitb@global.net.pg Website www.newirelandtourism.org.pg
Bougainville Tourism Office, Division of Commerce, Trade and Industry PO Box 38 Buka, Autonomous Region of Bougainville Tel/Fax 973 9613 Email bougainvilletourism@gmail.com or bougainvilletourism@yahoo.com Website www.bougainvilletourism.org.pg	Ecotourism Melanesia Ltd Sect 55 Lot 25 Lokua Avenue PO Box 531 Gordons, NCD Tel/Fax 325 3043/4860 Email ecomel@online.net.pg Website www.em.com.pg
Melanesian Tourist Services PO Box 707 Madang, MP Tel 424 1300, Fax 422 3543 Email info@mtspng.com Website www.mtspng.com	Trans Niugini Tours PO Box 371 Mt Hagen, WHP Tel 542 1438, Fax 542 2470 Email service@pngtours.com Website www.pngtours.com

Tourism contacts in PNG (contact details may change; always confirm before publishing)

Students from Divine Word University conducting tourism awareness on Karkar Island in Madang. This is one way for students to engage with local communities and impart what they have learnt at university to empower communities to organise for community development.

Unit 11.1 Activity 4: Community tourism – short-answer questions

1. Identify factors that will contribute to the success of community tourism.
2. Identify factors that will hinder community tourism.
3. What agreement or consent is needed at the village or community level for community tourism to progress?

Unit 11.1 Introduction to the Tourism Industry
Topic 5: Impacts of tourism

In Topic 5 we consider the implications of tourism and its environmental and economic impacts – the positives and the negatives.

Describing the impacts of tourism

As discussed in Topic 1, a tourism model consists of three essential elements, which can be summarised as follows: a tourist-generating region, a transit region and a tourist destination region. Each element of the model has its own level of impacts. We should remember that tourism takes place in an environment that combines human and natural elements. The human environment comprises economic, social and cultural factors and processes. The natural environment is made up of plants and animals and their habitats. These two environments are important when discussing the impacts of tourism.

The impacts of tourism are many-sided, often combining economic, sociocultural and environmental dimensions. Each tourism activity has its own pros and cons. The nature of a particular **tourism impact** is related to a variety of factors: the type of tourism activity, where and when it is taking place, **seasonality** (closely related to the climate and the annual calendar) and existing tourism infrastructure.

The economic concept of tourism is the sum total of **tourist expenditures** within the borders of a nation, political subdivision or transportation-centred economic area of neighbouring states or nations. Generally, positive economic impacts of tourism are:

- Employment.
- **Foreign exchange earnings**.
- Government income through tax **revenue**.
- Regional development through tourism infrastructure.

There are also negative impacts. Some of these are:

- **Inflation**.
- **Opportunity costs**.
- Over-dependence on tourism.
- **Terrorism** threats.
- Over-development of tourism infrastructure beyond the capacity of the site.
- Exhaustion of the host community's scarce resources through catering for growing demand.

Some developing countries have selected tourism as part of their approach to development, but they need to be aware that tourism development has both advantages and disadvantages. To understand the sociocultural impacts of tourism, we must firstly understand the meaning of the terms 'society' and 'culture'. Sociology is the study of society and is concerned with the study of people in groups, their interactions, attitudes and behaviour. Culture, on the other hand, is about how people interact as observed through social interactions, social relations and material artefacts. Interactions between the host community and tourists will have a major influence on the types of impacts. Positive sociocultural impacts may include:

- Hosts and visitors developing positive attitudes towards each other.
- Learning about each other's culture and **customs**.

- Reducing negative perceptions and **stereotypes**.
- Developing friendships.
- Developing pride, appreciation and understanding of each other's culture.
- Increasing self-esteem of hosts and tourists.
- Psychological satisfaction from interaction.
- Creation of employment.

Negative sociocultural impacts may include:

- Overcrowding in certain areas, causing stress for both tourists and residents.
- Decline in traditional farming activities.
- Over-dependence on tourism to sustain life.
- Conflict in value systems, and jealousy amongst residents when tourists are seen to be having a good time while residents are working.
- Seasonal nature of tourism forcing residents to modify their way of life for part of the year.
- Possibility of **acculturation** after longer-term, deeper contact between tourists and residents.

The environment, which is made up of both human and natural features, is increasingly being recognised as a key factor in tourism. Human settlements located in rural areas may have many attractions for tourists. The natural environment is also referred to as the physical environment and includes the landscape, features such as rivers, rocky outcrops and beaches, and the plants and animals (flora and fauna). The diagram below shows the breadth of the concept of 'the environment'.

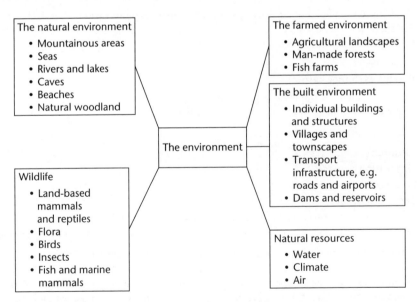

The concept of environment is broad in scope, encompassing both naturally occurring and human-made phenomena. Diverse aspects can interact with and affect each other, so by deliberately or accidentally changing one element we can sometimes cause unexpected consequences to other elements. Building a major road through a forest, for example, may disturb the migration and breeding patterns of some native animals. What are some steps we can take to ensure that our actions do not have unintended negative effects on the environment?

Positive environmental impacts of tourism may include:

- Measures to protect and conserve the natural environment.
- Establishment of national parks, wildlife management areas and reserves.
- Preservation of historic buildings and monuments.
- Income generation (from entrance fee charges) that can be used to maintain historical buildings, heritage sites and wildlife habitats.

Negative environmental impacts of tourism may include:

- Damage or disturbance to wildlife habitats.
- Creation of buildings and other structures that do not fit into the local environment.
- Littering.
- Congestion – overcrowding of people or traffic.
- Pollution of beaches and watercourses.

The nature of the activities in which tourists are engaged, where and when they happen, seasonality factors and the state of tourism infrastructure will greatly influence the impacts that tourism has on the generating region, the transit region and the destination region.

*Study the photograph and consider the ways in which the **selling** of arts and crafts can benefit Papua New Guineans. Are there any disadvantages? Are there any safeguards that you would like to see implemented, from the point of view of everyone involved in tourism?*

In what ways do our cultures attract tourists to PNG? How does tourism contribute to the promotion and maintenance of our traditional cultures? Does tourism contribute to sustainable cultural activities, or not?

In what ways does tourism contribute to environmental protection? Are there ways in which it might not protect our environment? How can we ensure that there is minimal damage to the natural environment while visitors have a good time?

Unit 11.1 Activity 5: Tourism impacts – short-answer questions

Identify positive and negative economic, sociocultural and environmental impacts of tourism from the perspective of a community affected by tourism.

Unit 11.2 Tourism in Papua New Guinea
Topic 1: Introduction – Tourism in Papua New Guinea

Tourism in Papua New Guinea is a growing industry. Our country's many attractions include culture, markets, festivals, diving, surfing, hiking, fishing and our unique flora and fauna. Unit 11.2 should enable students to achieve learning outcomes 1, 2, 3 and 4 (see Syllabus page 5). Topic 1 presents an introduction to tourism in our country. Students are expected to:
- Demonstrate an understanding of tourism at the local, national, regional and international level.
- Describe and explain the growth of local, national, regional and global tourism.
- Identify the role of tourism in the economic growth of a country.
- Demonstrate an understanding of the impact of tourism at individual, local, national, regional and global levels.

People generally agree that there is vast potential for tourism in Papua New Guinea. PNG as a tourist destination offers more varied tourism products and services than most other single destinations in the world.

PNG has benefited from a global tourism boom in the years from 2005 to 2010, from an annual average of 60 000 visitor arrivals to more than 100 000. Three factors that have contributed to this are a stable government and economy; positive rating of our government's performance by international rating agencies (partly influenced by better world **commodity** prices) leading to a positive destination image; and encouragement of foreign **investment**, such as in the exploration and development of petroleum and mining. Industries like the LNG (liquid natural gas) project bring more business travellers and foreign currency earnings and reserves. The *PNG Tourism Sector Review and Master Plan (2007–2017)* recognised that the development of the tourism industry in PNG is reliant on a partnership between government, industry and the people of PNG.

The three primary areas of tourism in PNG are culture, nature and adventure. But PNG also receives a large number of visitors who come for business purposes. This is evident in the August 2010 visitor arrivals summary analysis carried out by the Papua New Guinea Tourism Promotion Authority (PNGTPA):

Visitor arrivals in Papua New Guinea by purpose: August 2010 (source: PNGTPA, c. 2010). Upon arriving in PNG, every visitor completes an arrival card for PNG Customs. The information gathered includes the purpose of the visit. This pie chart summarises the information collected for August 2010.

As the following table shows, Australia is the main source market for visitors to PNG. This is because Australia is located closest to PNG (other than West Papuan Province of Indonesia), the two countries share historical, political and economic ties (whereby PNG receives the biggest portion of Australian aid) and there are Australian investments in PNG.

A comparison of the numbers of visitors to PNG from other source markets between August 2009 and August 2010 shows the following increases and decreases: New Zealand (+36%), Oceania (–16%), Japan (–5%), Asia (+26%), Europe (+37%), USA (+31%) and Africa (–4%). PNG recorded an 18% increase in visitor arrivals in August 2010 compared to same period in 2009.

Country	Bus	MICE	VFR	Hol	Empt	Edu	Other	Aug 2010	Aug 2009	Change	Change (%)
Australia	3504	75	437	1206	1155	23	12	6412	5646	+766	+14
New Zealand	364	11	19	78	114	1	3	590	435	+155	+36
Oceania	97	20	30	42	38	7	4	238	284	–46	–16
China	261	2	9	69	297	7	5	650	543	+107	+20
Japan	96	7	8	238	18	0	1	368	388	–20	–5
South Korea	53	0	4	35	11	0	0	103	99	+4	+4
Malaysia	206	1	16	65	136	3	1	428	382	+46	+12
Singapore	80	0	3	28	9	0	4	124	64	+60	+94
Philippines	268	6	30	47	394	13	5	763	679	+84	+12
Indonesia	72	1	5	14	57	0	1	150	117	+33	+28
India	101	1	6	23	84	5	2	222	122	+100	+82
Other Asia	79	1	6	63	56	0	2	207	103	+104	+101
United Kingdom	204	6	8	71	71	0	3	363	269	+94	+35
Germany	26	1	10	63	15	7	0	122	137	–15	–11
France	35	1	0	38	7	0	0	81	67	+14	+21
Netherlands	28	1	1	19	17	2	0	68	31	+37	+119
Other Europe	74	2	8	92	32	2	1	211	134	+77	+57
USA	340	7	33	255	124	12	11	782	598	+184	+31
Canada	83	1	6	22	37	3	1	153	120	+33	+28
Other America	18	0	0	8	5	0	0	31	20	+11	+55
Africa	41	0	4	9	20	0	0	74	62	+12	+19
Russia	35	0	2	16	4	0	0	57	30	+27	+90
Italy	10	1	3	81	5	0	0	100	59	+41	+69
Scandinavia	16	0	0	7	5	0	0	28	25	+3	+12
Chile	0	0	0	0	0	0	0	0	2	–2	–100
Israel	3	0	0	18	1	0	0	22	38	–16	–42
Total 2010	6094	145	648	2607	2712	85	56	12347	10454	+1893	+18
Total 2009	4777	210	468	2529	2381	52	37	10454			
Change	+1317	–65	+180	+78	+331	+33	+19	+1893			
Change (%)	+28	–31	+38	+3	+14	+63	+51	+18			

Abbreviations: Bus = Business; MICE = Meetings, Incentives, Conferences and Exhibitions; VFR = Visiting Friends and Relatives; Hol = Holiday; Empt = Employment; Edu = Education.

PNG visitor arrivals by country of origin: August 2010 compared to August 2009 (source: PNGTPA, c. 2010). Statistics like these enable governments and other interested parties to plan for the future.

PNG has a high return rate for visitors, indicating that visitors generally have a favourable experience here. Factors that make PNG attractive as a tourist destination include:

- PNG is generally removed from war, terrorism and major disease outbreaks. Although PNG has its own problems, many are local rather than nationwide and some are more perception than reality.
- PNG is seen as exotic, safe, friendly, unspoilt and full of new and exciting experiences.
- PNG can offer good travel **bargains**.
- The local people are generally regarded as friendly and hospitable.
- PNG is in the exotic category of **tourism destinations**, which may encourage travel agents and other providers in distant **traveller-generating regions** to promote PNG travel.
- There is increasing airline **competition**, discounted travel packages and better onward connections.
- PNG offers a diversity of tourism products and services, and has a pleasant tropical climate and predictable wet and dry weather patterns.
- PNG has enough international-standard facilities and services to cater to overseas delegates and to host international events.
- PNG offers unique experiences that cannot be found in other destinations.

Although PNG has great tourism potential, our tourism industry is still at the developing stage, with challenges and obstacles to overcome. Some of these may be addressed in the short term, while others are more for the long term. Examples include:

- Perception of law-and-order problems through media reporting and other sources.
- A highly unstable airline industry with frequent cancellations, delayed flights and high fares.
- Lack of high-quality and complimentary facilities (such as Internet access) at PNG airports and other locations.
- Long times taken to service aircraft, process visas, complete **immigration** and **quarantine** formalities and unload baggage.
- Multiple fees charged by different organisations to cruise ship companies, and expensive accommodation in hotels and resorts.
- Poor infrastructure such as roads in bad condition (e.g. the damaged and poorly maintained scenic Okuk–Highlands Highway), broken bridges and roads passing through rivers.
- Little reliable public transport; buses and taxis that are often crowded, dirty and in poor condition.
- Concern about quality of service.
- Inadequate printed or Internet information on tourist destinations and products, for customers both within PNG and overseas.
- Doubts about hygiene standards for food preparation in commercial outlets; limited variety of food in towns and rural locations.

The PNG government's strategy to address these challenges is multi-sectoral and bipartisan. This means that all sectors – whether private or government, institutional or individual, urban or rural – that control and influence tourism should work together and share the costs and benefits of operating tourism in this country. For example, one of the challenges listed above is the multiple fees charged by different organisations to cruise ships arriving at PNG. This could be constructively solved if the different departments communicated with each other.

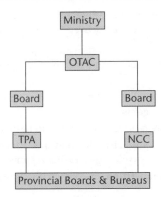

New structural framework under Ministry of Tourism, Arts and Culture

To administer the tourism industry nationwide, it is important to have the right structure, clearly delineating the responsibilities of the different government offices and NGOs involved. In 2008 the minister responsible for tourism, arts and culture initiated a review of the structure of the ministry to improve delivery of government policy. This diagram shows the new structure. The abbreviations are: OTAC = Office of Tourism, Arts and Culture; TPA = Tourism Promotions Authority; NCC = National Cultural Commission.

Under the new structure, the Ministry of Tourism, Arts and Culture (previously the Ministry of Culture and Tourism), headed by the minister, oversees the Office of Tourism, Arts and Culture (OTAC), headed by a director-general. The ministry endorses the policy directions for OTAC and associated agencies (the Tourism Promotion Authority, headed by a chief executive officer, and the National Cultural Commission, headed by an executive director). Each of these agencies has a separate board, made up of representatives of the tourism industry and associated government departments. The agencies maintain close communication with provincial boards and information bureaus to ensure that government policies are being implemented at the local level.

The ministry's endorsement of changes to the structural framework accords with the *Tourism Master Plan 2007–2017*, which advocates 'growing tourism as a sustainable industry'. This document states that on average, tourists spend K7000 each and therefore the industry needs serious government support. It also argues that the proposed structure is in line with the *PNG Development Strategic Plan 2010–2030*, which identifies agriculture, tourism and manufacturing as the economic sectors to drive broad-based economic growth. The structure also supports *Vision 2050*, which identifies seven key pillars that tourism development can help strengthen: human capital development; people empowerment; wealth creation; service delivery; a positive international image; environmental sustainability; and spiritual, cultural and community development. This can be achieved through different agencies and stakeholders working together.

It is predicted that the **tourism sector** will deliver 310 000 jobs in PNG by 2030, higher than any other sector of the economy.

Some tourism facts about PNG:

- PNG has close to 9000 plant species, found mostly in lowland rainforests.
- PNG forests grow at least 3000 different kinds of orchids, more than any other country.
- PNG has 700 species of birds, including more parrot, pigeon and kingfisher species than anywhere else in the world.
- PNG is home to 38 of the 43 known species of birds of paradise.
- Around 250 species of mammals live here, mostly bats and rats, but also marsupials such as the tree kangaroo.
- The world's largest butterfly – Queen Alexandra's birdwing (female) – and the second-largest – the Goliath birdwing – are both found in PNG.
- The Hercules moth – the largest moth in the world – lives in many parts of PNG.
- More than 800 different languages and cultures exist in PNG. This is about one-tenth of all the world's languages and one-third of the world's indigenous tongues.

Whilst the National Cultural Commission is responsible for matters relating to PNG's historical and contemporary culture, the PNGTPA is the lead agency responsible for marketing and promoting PNG as a desirable tourist destination. Marketing is done through the following channels:

- The Internet.
- Local mass media (print, visual and audio).
- Cooperative marketing efforts such as UNWTO, PATA, SPTO.
- International representative offices: Tokyo, Los Angeles, Frankfurt, Stockholm and Australia, in partnership with Air Niugini **general sales agent agreements**.
- Trade shows.
- Brochures.
- Visiting journalists.
- Travel trade programs.
- Other promotional material.

Tourism in PNG is at an embryonic stage, with most of its potential still untapped. The nation's cultural differences, rough terrain, inaccessibility, lack of tourism-specific awareness and education, and poor management of its development resources have all slowed the growth of tourism. One advantage is that PNG can learn from the experiences of other countries and avoid the pitfalls. Serious investment in tourism activities is needed as more of the country's natural resources are being rapidly depleted. PNG needs to focus on forms of tourism that can develop despite the constraints on many of the nation's resources.

The highland moss forest on PNG's scenic Highlands (Okuk) Highway. The highway provides exhilarating views for travellers. How can we protect the environment while allowing access for tourists?

Natural features such as limestone cliffs jutting out of the water attract tourists to PNG. Consider the various tourist activities that are related to water. How can we protect our waterways while enabling tourists to enjoy water activities as part of their experience?

Unit 11.2 Activity 1A: Tourism in Papua New Guinea – short-answer questions

1. Identify factors that contributed to the growth of visitor arrivals in PNG between 2005/06 and 2010.

2. Provide examples of tourism products (tourist attractions or activities) that relate to culture, nature and adventure.

3. Explain why PNG gets more visitors from Australia than from any other country.

4. Give an example of how the tourism industry in PNG can flourish as a result of partnership between the government, industry and people of PNG.

5. Describe how the PNG tourism industry can contribute towards achieving *Vision 2050*.

Unit 11.2 Activity 1B: Tourism in Papua New Guinea – short essay

Describe the tourism potential in your area by identifying both the attractive features and obstacles to tourism development, and how the latter can be rectified.

Unit 11.2 Tourism in Papua New Guinea
Topic 2: Tourist attractions in Papua New Guinea

In line with the Syllabus (pages 11–12), Topic 2 looks at what might make a destination attractive to tourists. In the context of PNG, these include factors such as culture, festivals, markets, diving, surfing, hiking and trekking.

A tourist attraction is a community, place, event, activity, phenomenon or item of interest that tourists visit, typically for its inherent or exhibited cultural value, historical significance, natural or built beauty, or entertainment potential.

There is a great variety of types of tourist attractions. They include mountains, beaches, islands and oceans, village communities, traditional rituals and ceremonies, wildlife, historical places, monuments, zoos, museums and art galleries, botanical gardens, buildings and structures (e.g. traditional houses, libraries, parliament house, skyscrapers, bridges), national parks and forests, and natural phenomena (e.g. volcanoes, animal migration, sunrises and sunsets). Many tourist attractions are also landmarks.

A tourist attraction is a **tourist product** that can be offered to tourists to satisfy their demand. A product is anything that can be offered to satisfy a need or a want. In order to effectively define what is a tourist attraction, it is important for a number of reasons to consider its essential elements. For this purpose, we can identify six elements (modified from Gunn, 1985) that define a tourist attraction:

1. *It is a named site.* A named attraction is easily identified so that people know about it. This is important for **itinerary** development and to ensure the attraction can be more easily found and identified by tourists when they visit.

2. *It has a nucleus.* A site has a centre of attraction that becomes the focus of tourist attention, and without which the site can lose its meaning and become less appealing for visitors. It is important to manage the site in such a way that this nucleus is protected.

3. *It has markers.* A marker is any information about the attraction. Without markers the attraction has less meaning. Markers are important in managing a site because through them tourists can learn about the attraction and respect it.

4. *It has an inviolate belt.* An area immediately surrounding the main attraction or nucleus is the 'inviolate belt', which protects the nucleus from damage or destruction. If visitors venture forward from the inviolate belt they may reduce the quality of the main attraction and eventually destroy it.

5. *It has a zone of closure.* The zone of closure is the area beyond the inviolate belt, which contains service facilities such as rest houses, toilets, information booths, souvenir shops, food and drink outlets and children's playgrounds. Some attractions may not have these facilities but they are important considerations in meeting tourists' expectations.

6. *It is the focus of visitor and management attention.* Management should focus its resources and attention on those attractions that are of particular interest to tourists, and which they have adequate resources to manage properly. These will then become a worthwhile investment. Managers do not have the capability to manage all possible attractions and tourists do not have the time or energy to see and do everything.

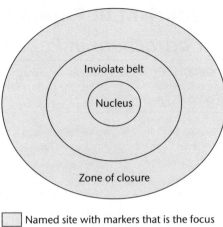

Named site with markers that is the focus
of visitor and management attention

Model of analysing a tourist attraction

One attraction may have several nuclei, which become the focus of visitor attention and the motivating factor for tourist travel. Markers are useful in that they inform tourists' decision making, helping draw tourists to the destination. A tourist's interest might initially be raised by markers about one particular nucleus, but after arriving at the site the tourist might discover several other nuclei (secondary nuclei). This makes the experience more worthwhile.

Tourist attractions are also important because they provide major symbols and images through which to promote a destination to the public. The image of any tourist destination is dependent on its mosaic of attractions, and the profile of visitors to a region will be partly determined by the attractions available.

Thus destinations become more popular if they have a variety of activities and attractions for tourists. This is based on the idea of **synergism**: *the 1 + 1 = 3 principle,* meaning that the combination is more attractive than the sum of its parts. In practice this means that all successful tourist attractions have a nucleus, and the more nuclei an attraction has, the more satisfying the experience for visitors.

For example, the diagram opposite is a floor plan of attractions found in the Madang Visitors and Cultural Bureau (MVCB). The MVCB facility is in itself an attraction. It has a fence surrounding its premises, a green lawn inside the fence and a small garden inside the gate – just in front of the museum. Adjoining the museum building to the left is a gift shop. Inside the museum there is the information centre, which provides brochures and other tourist information and assistance; the museum itself, displaying a variety of artefacts such as masks, carvings, clay pots, weapons, butterfly specimens and colonial history; and the theatre tower which contains theatre costumes. If tourists require further assistance this is also available. The combination of all of these activities and attractions makes the visitor experience worthwhile and satisfying. If we were to remove any of its elements the MVCB would lose much of its appeal and might no longer be exciting for tourists.

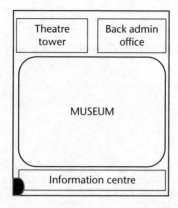

Synergism in action at the Madang Visitors and Cultural Bureau

To further demonstrate the importance of tourist attractions, the PNG Tourism Promotion Authority in its June 2008 arrivals summary reported a 17 per cent increase in visitors from Australia. This was due to more Australians wanting to walk the Kokoda Trail. The report stated that in 2007 the Kokoda Trek alone generated K25 million, out of a total tourist expenditure of K300 million, a reflection of the cultural significance of this walk and the economic contribution of tourist attractions as major drawcards.

The attractions sector in PNG will gain momentum as improvements are made to existing attractions and new attractions are developed, for example, development of the Ela Beach Park, construction of the new Papuan Hotel in Port Moresby and Gazelle International Hotel in East New Britain, and development of the proposed marine park on the north coast of Madang. These, combined with further development of natural and cultural attractions, can create new interest and excitement for tourists. Another advantage of many PNG tourist attractions is that they are found in rural towns and remote areas; this could help create employment and motivation for rural people.

The following is a summary of principles for the development and management of successful visitor attractions:

1. Resource elements – An attraction needs a striking or distinctive physical or cultural resource as its core.
2. Public conceptions or understanding – The attraction should be readily understood and appreciated by the public, or offer interpretive facilities.
3. Visitor activities – The attraction will provide scope for visitor experience, and offer activities that are responsible and accessible and that excite the public imagination.
4. Inviolate belt – The attraction will be presented in a context that preserves the resource and enables the visitor to appreciate and reflect on its qualities.
5. Services zone – The attraction will provide visitor services (toilets, shopping, etc.), but not to the detriment of the resource.
6. Price – The attraction will be priced to reflect the relative quality of the resource, its management, visitors' length of stay and a healthy return on public or private investment.

Consider the flora and fauna of Papua New Guinea. Make a list of those plants and animals that you believe would attract tourists to our country. What factors should be taken into account to enable tourists to experience our flora and fauna? How might our flora and fauna be damaged by tourism and what safeguards can you suggest?

A traditional mumu. How important is food in the tourism business? What kind of food experiences do you think visitors to our country would enjoy?

Unit 11.2 Activity 2A: Tourism in Papua New Guinea – short-answer questions

1. Identify tourism attractions in the following categories:
   a. Natural sites.
   b. Natural events.
   c. Cultural sites:
      i. Historical.
      ii. Contemporary culture.
      iii. Economic.
      iv. Recreational facilities.
      v. Shopping.
   d. Cultural events:
      i. Sporting events.
      ii. Historical commemorations.
      iii. World fairs.
      iv. Festivals.
2. Give examples of the development of new types of attractions.

Unit 11.2 Activity 2B: Tourism in Papua New Guinea – field report

Visit a nearby tourist attraction and write a field report identifying the six essential elements that make it a tourist attraction.

Unit 11.2 Tourism in Papua New Guinea
Topic 3: Issues – security and safety; transport

The Syllabus (page 13) highlights some of the issues to consider when tourists visit our country: security and safety for example, and different forms of transport. Topic 3 looks at some of these. Students are then invited to prepare their own case study that considers some of the issues explored in this Unit.

Security and safety

The 11 September 2001 terrorist attacks in the United States of America sent shock waves of fear around the world. The USA, despite having the best defence systems in the world, could not prevent this catastrophe; that realisation raised the question of security and safety to a whole new level. Some of the more obvious security measures in most countries include the use of scanning machines and sniffer dogs at airports and CCTV cameras in **public places** such as hotels. Immigration laws have become stricter in many countries, more closely screening people who are travelling or intend to travel to a country.

Although safety and security are real concerns among citizens and travellers alike, a contentious issue is perception versus reality. For instance, tribal fights sometimes occur in the Highlands; reports of these fights create a perception in many people's minds that the Highlands (or indeed all of PNG) is not a safe place to visit. But the reality is that such tribal fights involve only those communities in conflict; they do not affect the day-to-day business of other people, and other provinces are safe to visit. Unfortunately, perceptions form part of people's belief systems, which influence their attitudes, and in this case have caused PNG to lose tourists. Thus the issue of safety and security must be addressed if potential tourists are to feel confident that they will be safe when visiting PNG.

Following are some examples that link tourism to doubts about safety and security:

- Tourists being robbed, mugged or assaulted.
- Tourists getting caught in the crossfire in a conflict, e.g. a bus carrying tourists along a road, across which two warring parties are exchanging gun shots.
- Tourists losing valuables from a guest house.
- A transport crash that kills passengers, including foreign tourists.
- Unaccompanied tourists getting lost, even if they are eventually discovered and rescued.
- Tourists getting sick from food poisoning.

A distinguishing factor in all these examples is that tourists or their property are affected. If these events occurred but did not directly affect any tourists (for example a plane crashed but there were no international tourists on board, or some valuable hotel equipment was stolen from a hotel), the perception might be different. That being said, tourists' overall sense of their safety and security might still suffer, because of perceptions. Even if no tourists were directly affected, air travel in this country might be seen as generally unsafe and hotels as lacking adequate security.

In most countries, governments issue travel warnings or alerts to citizens intending to travel abroad. Host countries and agents also provide information for those intending to visit.

Following are examples of efforts made by the Papua New Guinea Tourism Promotion Authority (PNGTPA) and other entities to ensure the safety and security of visitors in PNG:

- Health information is advertised on the PNGTPA website; people over one year of age travelling from or through infected areas must get certification of vaccination against yellow fever or cholera; anti-malarial preparations should be taken before arriving and during a stay in PNG.
- Air Niugini airline seats contain laminated instructions for in-flight exercises and other safety and security features; safety demonstrations by flight attendants; safety information in the in-flight Air Niugini *Paradise* magazine.
- Most accommodation establishments display maps of the building and directional signs for emergency exits, and provide safety tips and advice. Some accommodations employ security **personnel** on-site; major hotels provide security deposit boxes or safes to store guests' valuables.
- Tour companies employ guides to accompany tourists around sites of interest. They also provide meet-and-greet services, make travel arrangements and provide helpful information on topics such as:
  - Weather, dress codes and time zones – including the best travel times.
  - Health and safety.
  - Location and opening times of major support facilities such as banks, post offices, shops, chemists and markets.
  - Emergency contact names and numbers.
  - Recommended places to visit or things to do.
  - Customs and quarantine, electricity, currency and driving.
  - Geographical information.
  - Cultural norms and behaviours.
  - What to bring along.
- Operators make efforts to have clean water, utensils and facilities; fresh products; well-trained personnel with uniforms and IDs; first-aid kits or a medical attendant; clear tracks and signage; designated areas; emergency and other useful contact numbers; maps and schedules; instructors or guide; security equipment or personnel on-site; properly working machines and other equipment; regular fit-for-use checks of all equipment; and regular staff training.

If the safety and security of tourists in PNG are not looked after properly, the following could result:

- Negative destination image and word-of-mouth feedback, leading to loss of visitor arrivals.
- Fear and uncertainty in the minds of potential travellers, also leading to loss of visitor arrivals.
- Slow-down in domestic and foreign investment.
- **Principals** (companies that own facilities for visitor use, e.g. airlines and accommodations) lose business.
- Loss of markets for rural farmers, artefact and handcraft sellers.
- Governments lose tax revenue.
- Loss of foreign exchange earnings.
- Rise in cost of operation and destination costs to rebuild image and reputation.

It is important for safety and security information to be accessed by tourists before they arrive in PNG. Within PNG, such information must be displayed clearly and prominently. It is the responsibility of everyone – including tourists – to take reasonable care for their own and others' welfare. Absolute safety and security cannot be guaranteed in any destination.

Air Niugini has an excellent safety record, with only three accident incidents ever recorded by the Aviation Safety Network. Research Air Niuguni's weekly flight schedule and consider why some people would say that Air Niuguni's safety record is 'impeccable and against all the odds'. Do you agree? Give reasons for your answer.

Unit 11.2 Activity 3A: Tourism in Papua New Guinea – security and safety

1. Identify safety and security measures in the following cases:
   a. You are guiding a tourist for a bushwalk.
   b. A tourist checks in at your guest house.
   c. A tourist is interested in doing canoeing.
   d. You are preparing meals for your guests.
2. The village councillor and other elders are convinced that tourism is the best development option for your community. What local safety and security concerns need addressing?

Transport

Transportation is an essential component of the tourism and hospitality industry. Transportation networks bring the tourist to the destination to buy products and services. Today's tourism experience would be inconceivable without transportation. Establishing an effective, modern transport system in PNG is crucial to all growth and development, including tourism development.

The three modes of transport are air, water and land. Inbound tourists use all three modes to reach PNG, although air transport is by far the most common (international arrivals of tourists on cruise ships and via road from Indonesia are minimal). Air travel is also widely used within PNG, largely because of our distinctive **geography**. It has contributed to development and improved communication by enabling travel to isolated communities, over rugged terrain, and to some of the world's most exotic and untouched tourism resources.

Air transport companies in PNG include Air Niugini, Airlines PNG, MAF and Travel Air. There are also helicopters, small-scale airplane operators and charters. The major international operators are Air Niugini (which partners with Qantas on Australian routes) and Airlines PNG (privately owned). Of the two, Air Niugini (the national airline, wholly owned by the PNG government through the Independent Public Business Corporation) has the majority market share. The table below lists the Air Niugini and Airlines PNG fleets, brief descriptions and destinations covered.

Aircraft (Air Niugini PX)	Aircraft information
B767-33AER	Manufacturer: Boeing; aircraft type: B767-300R; length: 59.94 m; wingspan: 47.57 m; power plant: two PW4000; cruising speed: 857 km/h; normal altitude: 11 000–12 000 m; standard seating capacity: 214 passengers; range: 8100 km.
F100	Manufacturer: Fokker; aircraft type: F100; length: 35.53 m; wingspan: 28.08 m; power plant: two Rolls Royce Tay 650; cruising speed: 780 km/h; normal altitude: 11 000 m; standard seating capacity: 98 passengers; range: 3000 km.
Q400 Next Generation	Manufacturer: Bombardier; aircraft type: Q400 Next Gen; length: 32.83 m; wingspan: 28.42 m; power plant: two Pratt & Whitney PW150A; cruising speed: 667 km/h; normal altitude: 7500 m; standard seating capacity: 74 passengers; range: 2404 km.
Q400	Manufacturer: Bombardier; aircraft type: Q400; length: 32.83 m; wingspan: 28.42 m; power plant: two Pratt & Whitney PW150A; cruising speed: 667 km/h; normal altitude: 7500 m; standard seating capacity: 70 passengers; range: 2084 km.
DASH 8-Q315	Manufacturer: Bombardier; aircraft type: DASH 8-Q315; length: 25.7 m; wingspan: 24.4 m; power plant: two Pratt & Whitney PW123E; cruising speed: 510 km/h; normal altitude: 7500 m; standard seating capacity: 50 passengers; range: 1700 km.
DHC-8-202	Manufacturer: Bombardier; aircraft type: DHC-8-202; length: 22.25 m; wingspan: 25.89 m; power plant: two Pratt & Whitney PW123D; cruising speed: 550 km/h; normal altitude: 7600 m; standard seating capacity: 36 passengers; range: 1800 km.

Aircraft (Airlines PNG CG)	Aircraft information
De Havilland DASH 8	Renowned for being a leader in its class for short-field performance; 2 + 2 seating configuration, full galley, large baggage compartment, full-size toilet, latest safety features including weather radar, EGPWS, TCAS II and radar altimeter; various configurations including 36-seat passenger interior, 28-seat interior, 20-seat interior or as a total freighter; in-flight DVD system; power plant: two 1490 kW Pratt & Whitney Canada PW120A turboprops driving four bladed constant-speed Hamilton standard propellers; performance: maximum cruising speed 490 km/h; long-range cruising speed: 440 km/h; initial rate of climb: 1560 ft/min; range with full passenger load, fuel and reserves: 1520 km; range with a 2720 kg payload: 2040 km; weights: operating empty weight: 10 250 kg; maximum take-off: 15 650 kg; dimensions: wingspan: 25.91 m; length: 22.25 m; height: 7.49 m; wing area: 54.35 sq. m; capacity: flight crew of three; typical passenger seating for 37 at four abreast and 79 cm pitch.
De Havilland Twin Otter 300	Although it is not pressurised, the Twin Otter is excellent for short-sector operations and makes a first-class passenger and freight aircraft. Power plant: two 460 kW P&WC PT6A-27; performance: maximum cruising speed: 338 km/h; initial rate of climb: 1600 ft/min; range with 1135 kg payload: 1297 km; range with a 860 kg payload and wing tanks: 1705 km; weights: operating empty: 3363 kg; maximum take-off: 5670 kg; dimensions: wingspan 19.81 m; length: 15.77 m, or 15.09 m for seaplane variants; height: 5.94 m; wing area: 39.02 sq. m; capacity: flight crew of two; standard commuter interior seats 20 at three abreast and 76 cm pitch. Can be configured as an executive transport, freighter, aerial ambulance or survey aircraft.

Destination (Air Niugini PX)	Country
Cairns, Brisbane, Sydney	Australia
Honiara	Solomon Islands
Manila	Philippines
Narita	Japan
Singapore	Singapore
Hong Kong	China
Nadi	Fiji

Destination (Airlines PNG CG)	Country
Cairns, Brisbane	Australia

Air Niugini and Airlines PNG fleet and international destinations
(sources: Air Niugini 2012 & Airlines PNG 2006–07)

Types of water transport used by international and local tourists in PNG include cruise ships (e.g. MV *Sepik Spirit*, owned by Trans Niugini Tours, and MV *Kalibobo Spirit*, owned by Melanesian Tourist Services, based in PNG), live-aboard vessels, boats, motorised canoes, yachts, cargo ships and passenger ships. Examples of land transport used by local and international tourists in PNG include walking, trekking, PMV buses, hire cars, taxis and bicycles. The road transport infrastructure in PNG is inadequate, both in terms of maintenance and nationwide connectivity. This leads to road transport inaccessibility for tourists and locals alike, high costs and loss of potential revenue for industry operators. PNG's water transport services are also inadequate, infrequent, overcrowded and not conducive for international tourists. Cruise boats in PNG are adversely affected by fluctuating tourist numbers and cancellations, while factors such as negative international and local media publicity further reduce tourist interest.

A tourist's choice of transport depends on:

- Price.
- Destination.
- Time – how much is available?
- Reason – visiting family and friends, business or leisure?
- Departure points – how easy it is to get there?
- Convenience – e.g. discounted travel packages.

Many **tour operators** overseas will try to encourage more people to travel by combining travel packages (e.g. air transport + accommodation + land tours) and offering discounts. They will book flights from more accessible regional airports – either direct to the final destination or to one of the major international airports – for smooth onward **long-haul** connections.

The benefits of good transportation systems include:

- Bringing tourists to the destination to enjoy cultural, natural and other tourism products and services.
- Tourists meeting locals and other visitors to the destination, with interactions and exchange leading to understanding, peace and prosperity.
- Tax revenue for the national government.
- Income for principals (operators of airlines and other businesses).
- Employment and income for workers.
- Foreign exchange earnings.
- Creating a positive image of a friendly destination.
- Convenience.

The consequences to PNG's tourism industry if tourists' transport needs are not met include:

- Customer dissatisfaction.
- Rise in visitor complaints and spread of negative word-of-mouth feedback.
- Negative perception of the industry and destination.
- Drop in visitor arrivals.
- Loss of revenue.
- Loss of jobs.
- Loss of opportunities for education and awareness of other cultures.

In order to stimulate growth in tourist numbers, PNG's transportation operators must maintain their infrastructure in good condition; adhere to strict laws to ensure passenger safety and security; shorten handling and processing times; and coordinate with government departments and agencies to agree upon standard measures (e.g. the collection and remittance of fees charged to cruise ships). Problems caused by unreliable transportation, lack of competition and landowner issues need creative and innovative solutions.

A dug-out wooden canoe with motor is a typical form of water transport for tourists on the famous Sepik River. These long canoes can carry both passengers and cargo, including the weight of a fuel drum to power the motor. Compare this with the MV Sepik Spirit. *What might be the attractions of each kind of transport to potential tourists?*

The luxurious cruise boat MV Sepik Spirit, *owned and operated by Trans Niugini Tours, conducts tours to villages along the Sepik River. Compare this with the dug-out canoe. What might be the costs and benefits for the local Papua New Guineans who have contact with either of these two forms of transport?*

Unit 11.2 Activity 3B: Tourism in Papua New Guinea – short-answer questions

1. List three transport modes that international tourists would use to enter PNG.
2. What transport modes can tourists use to arrive at your place?
3. What suggestions can you make for the improvement of transport modes that you know tourists use?
4. What are the costs and benefits of improving or not improving tourist transport modes?

Unit 11.2 Activity 3C: Tourism in Papua New Guinea – case study: Austria–PNG group tour

A group of 15 Austrians book through Media Tours, a travel agent in Salzburg, for a two-week tour of various destinations in PNG. They would like to travel from Salzburg in Austria to Frankfurt in Germany, then to Singapore and directly on to Port Moresby without spending a transit night in between. In PNG they would like to spend time in these locations:

- One day in Port Moresby (arrival date).
- Three days in Madang.
- Four days in Kumul Lodge, Enga.
- Four days in Ambunti Lodge, Sepik River.
- One day in Surfside Lodge, Wewak.
- Leave Wewak for Port Moresby and on to international connection (departure date).

1. Create a small tour plan for the group by identifying the activities and transport needs for each day and each location.
2. As part of your case study, discuss some of the issues covered in this Unit.

Unit 11.2 Activity 3D: Tourism in Papua New Guinea – transport

Research the different types of aircraft and numbers of each type of aircraft operated by the different airlines in Papua New Guinea.

Unit 11.3 Our Neighbours and Tourism
Topic 1: Tourism and neighbouring countries

In Unit 11.3 students consider the importance of tourism in relation to Papua New Guinea's neighbours. Many Papua New Guineans visit countries close by, such as Australia, New Zealand, West Papua, Singapore and the Solomon Islands, and people from those countries visit PNG. Students are expected to:

- Demonstrate an understanding of the importance of tourism at the local, national, regional and international levels.
- Describe and explain the growth of local, national, regional and international tourism.
- Demonstrate an understanding of the impact of tourism at individual, local, national, regional and global levels.
- Communicate tourism information in a variety of ways and settings.

Introduction to regional tourism

The Asia-Pacific is said to be the most dynamic regional tourism market in the world. Between 1990 and 2000 alone, the number of international tourist trips in the region doubled. By 1999, the region accounted for 16 per cent of all international tourist trips globally. The major contribution is **intraregional** travel (within the Asia-Pacific) rather than **inter-regional** travel (between Asia-Pacific and other regions). The UNWTO divides the Asia-Pacific region into four zones:

- North-East Asia (China, Japan, Korea and Taiwan).
- South-East Asia (Cambodia, Indonesia, Malaysia, Philippines, Singapore, Thailand and Vietnam).
- Oceania (Australia, Fiji, Micronesia, New Zealand, Papua New Guinea, Samoa, Tonga and Tuvalu).
- South Asia (Bangladesh, India, Iran, Nepal, Pakistan and Sri Lanka)

Some aspects that make the region's diversity attractive to tourists are:

- It is large: it stretches more than 15 000 kilometres from west to east and over 13 000 kilometres from north to south.
- It is diverse, taking in some of the richest, well-developed countries and some of the poorest countries in the world, with different lifestyles and costs of living.
- The climate and geography range from temperate to tropical, desert in some places to several hundred centimetres of rain a year, from flatlands to snow-capped mountains, from sparse vegetation on the coast to thick forests, from mere sand and a few coconut trees to rich land and marine biodiversity.
- It contains every major religion of the world and hundreds of languages and dialects.
- It has countries with highly developed tourism infrastructure and others considered exotic and untouched.
- The rapid growth of Asia-Pacific economies, starting with Japan and Australia, followed by the opening up of China's economy, then India's emergence as an economic superpower, all boosted tourism within the region.
- The PATA (Pacific Asia Travel Association) effectively promotes and markets the region as a desirable tourist region to benefit its members.

- The location in the region of several **gateway airports** (e.g. Singapore and Hong Kong) ensures fast connectivity time and smooth onward journey connections; the presence of some of the world's leading airlines (e.g. Singapore Airlines) is also favourable.
- Generally the region is free from some of the world's worst problems, and has developed a reputation for personal service and smiling and hospitable people.

PNG specifically fits into and is closely associated with the South Pacific region. PNG is a member of the South Pacific Tourism Organisation (SPTO), which promotes tourism interests within the South Pacific region to its member countries, which include Cook Islands, Fiji, French Polynesia (Tahiti), New Caledonia, Kiribati, Niue, Samoa, Solomon Islands, Tonga, Tuvalu and Vanuatu. This region can be further subdivided into three sub-regions: Polynesia, Micronesia and Melanesia. All have considerable internal diversity.

The first two sub-regions (Polynesia and Micronesia) account for 16% of the regional population and are characterised by small island entities separated by enormous expanses of ocean. Polynesia covers an area of 8639 square kilometres and Micronesia covers 3097 square kilometres. Both sub-regions experience land shortages, higher population densities (partly due to land shortages) and in some instances a higher level of human-induced environmental degradation, both on land and at sea. By comparison, Melanesia comprises large islands clustered into relatively compressed archipelagos that account for 97.9% (542 230 square kilometres) of all land in the region. It is distinguished from the other two sub-regions by its variety of landforms, relatively undisturbed habitat, high levels of biodiversity and the presence of indigenous communities. Each of the three sub-regions is named after its indigenous racial group. These were some of the last groups of people in the world to experience colonisation and then post-colonisation (decolonisation); although this has resulted in intermixture and acculturation the people have held strongly to their cultural roots. This is evident in cultural practices such as language, exchanges, relationships, art forms and land tenure systems, although other **attributes**, such as religion and economics, have undergone profound changes.

The South Pacific faces high fertility rates, steady population increase, threats from modern diseases and natural calamities, resource pressures, over-dependency and political instability. The lure of foreign investment and Western pressures to modernise the economy have caused tensions with traditional values and systems of organisation and resource allocation; this has prompted criticism from foreigners and has resulted in poor international rankings for many South Pacific states.

Tourism in the South Pacific region from 1988 to 1993, as shown in the table below, shows major contributions in tourist numbers by inter-regional travel, i.e. travel from outside the region (e.g. North America, Europe and Japan) to the South Pacific, specifically to SPTO member countries. Comparing intraregional to inter-regional travel, the ratio is 1:1.1 on average, or 46.6% to 53.4% average contribution of tourist inflows into the region between this period.

	1988	1989	1990	1991	1992	1993
Intraregional:						
Australia and New Zealand	213478	262178	263193	253526	264983	256767
%	36.8	39.3	38.2	38.5	37.8	34.5
Pacific Islands	54268	61316	66127	57284	61555	67410
%	9.3	9.2	9.6	8.7	8.8	9.1

	1988	1989	1990	1991	1992	1993
Sub-total	267746	323494	329320	310810	326538	324177
%	46.1	48.4	47.8	47.2	46.6	43.5
Inter-regional:						
North America	150988	133595	128195	116155	121447	139913
%	26.0	20.0	18.6	17.7	17.3	18.8
Europe	106779	121901	133983	131318	141215	162734
%	18.4	18.3	19.5	20.0	20.2	21.9
Japan	28178	54210	68453	71833	82042	87183
%	4.9	8.1	9.9	10.9	11.7	11.7
Other countries	26905	34641	28684	27703	29425	30577
%	4.6	5.2	4.2	4.2	4.2	4.1
Sub-total	312850	344347	359315	347009	374129	420407
%	53.9	51.6	52.2	52.8	53.4	56.5
Grand Total	580596	667841	688635	657819	700667	744584
%	100.0	100.0	100.0	100.0	100.0	100.0

Intraregional and inter-regional tourist flows in the SPTO region, 1988–1993
(source: SPTO & TCSP c. 1993b)

	$US million					
	1988	1989	1990	1991	1992	1993
Cook Islands	15	15	16	21	27	31
Fiji	131	199	227	211	223	251
French Polynesia	157	138	171	150	170	164
Kiribati	1	1	1	1	1	1
Marshall Islands	[na]	[na]	[na]	3	3	3
New Caledonia	64	86	94	94	93	95
Niue	-	-	-	-	-	-
Papua New Guinea	25	40	41	41	49	45
Solomon Islands	5	5	4	5	12	6
Tonga	7	9	9	10	9	9
Tuvalu[a]	n/a	n/a	n/a	n/a	n/a	n/a
Vanuatu	11	16	22	25	30	31
Western Samoa	18	19	20	18	17	21
Total	434	528	605	579	634	658

[a] Less than US$500 000 – not applicable

Foreign exchange earnings from tourism in SPTO countries, 1988–1993
(source: SPTO & TCSP c. 1993a)

Pacific state	Population[a]	GDP (US$ million)[b]	Tourist arrivals[c]
Cook Islands	14 000	86.5	78 300
Fiji	832 400	1 900.0	430 800
Kiribati	87 400	70.0	3 700
Marshall Islands	56 600	64.2	5 400
Micronesia (FMS)	107 500	222.1	18 200
Nauru	12 300	60.0	Less than 1 000
Niue	1 600	7.6	2 700
Palau	20 700	127.0	63 300
Papua New Guinea	5 520 000	4 400.0	56 200
Samoa	177 700	316.0	92 300
Solomon Islands	450 000	394.0	5 000
Tonga	98 300	131.0	40 100
Tuvalu	9 600	13.0	1 500
Vanuatu	204 100	247.0	50 400
Total	7 592 200	8 038.4	848 900

[a] *2004, except Solomon Islands, Tonga and Vanuatu (2003); Kiribati, Marshall Islands, Micronesia and Papua New Guinea (2002); Nauru (2001).*

[b] *2004, except Solomon Islands (2003); Cook Islands, Marshall Islands and Micronesia (2002); Nauru and Tuvalu (2001); Niue (2000).*

[c] *2003, except Marshall Islands (2001).*

Economic indicators of South Pacific countries, 2004 (source: PRO€INVEST c. 2004)

At the regional level, the South Pacific is over-represented as an inbound tourist destination, having only 0.13% of the world's population but attracting 0.5% of all international visits. It is also important to note that the internal distribution of tourism is highly skewed, being dominated by inbound rather than domestic tourism. There is also an unequal distribution of inbound tourist numbers and tourist revenue between countries, as the preceding tables show. In 1993 the top three Pacific countries in foreign exchange earnings were Fiji with US$251 million (K511.7 million), French Polynesia with US$164 million (K334.3 million) and New Caledonia with US$95 million (K195.3 million).

Some of the small island nations, such as Kiribati, Marshall Islands, Niue and Tuvalu, recorded less than US$5 million in foreign exchange earnings. Interestingly, some of these received more **tourist arrivals** than the size of their own population. Tourism made quite a contribution to the **gross domestic product** (GDP) of countries like Cook Islands (64 300 more tourist arrivals than population size); Niue (1100 more tourist arrivals than population size); and Palau (42 600 more tourist arrivals than population size). These figures record tourist arrivals, not necessarily the numbers of inbound tourists in those countries; they may include a large proportion of return visitors.

Problems faced by small island economies in trying to attract economic development from tourism include:

* Isolation.
* Lack of infrastructure and accommodation.
* Scarcity of freehold land.
* Lack of interest among potential investors.
* Distance from long-haul markets, thus increasing travel costs.
* Limited international air access.
* Insufficient marketing.

Some positive factors that attract tourists to this region include:

* Unspoiled nature and culture.
* Diverse tourism products and experiences, targeting **niche markets**.
* Effective marketing by regional organisations such as PATA and SPTO.
* A reputation as exotic and untouched.

For these and other reasons, most Pacific Island states have chosen tourism as a development tool to help them achieve national economic sustainability. Developing tourism as a sustainable industry for our region requires a broad perspective that encompasses governments, **special interest groups**, investors, local people and their resources, tourists and marketers. Ensuring a quality experience for visitors, benefits that are shared among all stakeholders, and enhancement of the integrity and quality of the resource will contribute to sustaining the industry for future generations.

The South Pacific Tourism Organisation (SPTO) effectively promotes its members and the South Pacific region as a desirable tourist destination. What are the advantages of PNG being part of SPTO? Are there any disadvantages?

The Asia-Pacific region, with its tropical climate, sunny skies, clear blue oceans, white sand beaches and friendly people, is a haven for tourists. How would you promote PNG in this context? What ways can you think of to promote the special experiences that PNG alone can offer while still being part of the Asia-Pacific region?

Unit 11.3 Activity 1A: Our neighbours and tourism – short-answer questions

1. Why is the Asia-Pacific region said to be the most dynamic regional tourism market in the world?
2. List positive factors that cause tourists to visit the South Pacific.
3. List factors that may prevent tourists from visiting the South Pacific.

Unit 11.3 Activity 1B: Our neighbouring countries

Copy and complete the table below with examples of countries in each region.

Region	Country
South Asia	
Oceania	
Polynesia	
Micronesia	
North-East Asia	
South-East Asia	
Melanesia	

Unit 11.3 Activity 1C: Our neighbouring countries – relative importance

1. Refer to the table 'Intraregional and inter-regional tourist flows in the SPTO region, 1988–1993' on pages 56–57 and rank PNG's neighbouring countries in descending order based on the number of tourist arrivals. Would you predict that the picture will be the same in 20 years' time? Give reasons for your answer.

2. Refer to the table 'Foreign exchange earnings from tourism in SPTO countries, 1988–1993' on page 57 and rank PNG's neighbouring countries in descending order based on foreign exchange earnings. Would you predict that the picture will be the same in 20 years' time? Give reasons for your answer.

Unit 11.3 Our Neighbours and Tourism
Topic 2: Fiji, Vanuatu and Cook Islands – case studies in tourism

Having examined some of the elements that characterise tourism as an industry, and some of the related issues, we now look at three neighbouring countries in which tourism is particularly important: Fiji, Vanuatu and Cook Islands.

Tourism in Fiji: a case study

Fiji, which is part of Oceania, is an island group in the South Pacific Ocean, about two-thirds of the way from Hawaii to New Zealand (18°S and 175°E). It is a member of the South Pacific Tourism Organisation and the location of SPTO's headquarters. The capital city is Suva, on Viti Levu, Fiji's main and largest island. A former British colony, Fiji is now a republic, having gained independence in 1970.

Fiji is made up of 332 islands, of which 110 are inhabited. Its estimated population of 0.89 million people comprises Indigenous Fijians (57.3%), Indian (37.6%), Rotuman (1.2%), with Europeans, Chinese and other Pacific Islanders making up the remaining 3.9%. With a land area of 18 274 square kilometres and a coastline of 1129 kilometres, it has a population density of 42 persons per square kilometre and in 2011 had an estimated GDP per capita of US$4600 (K9378). Its economy is supported by tourism, sugar, fishing, gold, timber, coconuts and manufacturing, the principal **exports** being sugar, clothing, fish, gold and timber. It encourages multiculturalism and several religions practise in Fiji.

With more than 6000 tourist rooms, Fiji is the most developed of the Pacific Islands, attracting 40% of the aggregate one million visitor arrivals in the region in 2003. It originally based its tourism development on its main natural attributes: the coastal environment and climate. With more than 300 islands, Fiji can offer a range of facilities, from conventional large-scale resorts on the main islands to exclusive resorts on smaller islands. Fiji is now expanding and diversifying its product offering, by drawing upon the country's cultural and natural resources. Ecotourism is seen as an attractive option for sharing the benefits of tourism with those islands that have not significantly benefited previously. Key to Fiji's tourism growth is foreign investment.

Although military coups in Fiji have caused tensions and uncertainty amongst some potential travellers and local businesses, several factors have contributed to a revival in tourism investment, including:

- The return of political stability, accompanied by positive assurances by political leaders to citizens and visitors.
- Government policy support and incentives for tourism development.
- Strong liquidity in the financial system, enabling borrowing for development.
- Well-developed tourism and support infrastructure.
- Increased marketing budgets for the Fiji Visitors Bureau.
- An increase in airline capacity.

- Major brands investing in Fiji, such as the Accor (Sofitel), Marriott and Hilton developments.
- Inter-island cruising with luxury cruise ships.

Foreign investment is welcomed by Fiji's tourism industry, as it is a major source of the capital required for building hotels and resorts. Foreigners may invest in almost all facets of the industry, either in their own right or in partnership with locals. These opportunities include:

- Hotel and resort development.
- Cruise operations.
- Tour and transportation operations.
- Distribution.
- Shopping and trade.
- Leisure and entertainment.
- Ecotourism.

There are also opportunities for Fijian **entrepreneurs** to invest in smaller-scale accommodation developments, many of which cater for the backpacker and **niche market segments** (e.g. star-gazing and island trekking).

Highlighted below are some brief facts about tourism in Fiji (as presented by the Fiji Bureau of Statistics and the Tourism Council of the South Pacific (TCSP), and covering the period 1990 to 1997).

- In 1997 Fiji experienced a growth rate in tourist arrivals of 5.9%, with total tourist arrivals of 359 441 in 1997 compared to 278 996 in 1990. Its major source markets were Australia, New Zealand, Japan, USA, UK, Pacific Islands, other Europe, other Asia, Canada and Germany.
- Purpose of visit was as follows: vacation (80.9%); business (7.8%); VFR (visiting friends and relatives) (5.6%); other purpose (5.8%). Fiji has generally experienced steady growth and consistent patterns, despite some small decreases in particular markets.
- Seasonality of arrivals: there is no pronounced seasonality in tourist arrivals in Fiji, although there was better performance in the latter half of the year.
- Visitors from most markets stayed for an average of 8.3 days.
- By the end of 1997 Fiji offered 220 hotels, with a total capacity of 5861 rooms; the majority of guest nights were spent by overseas visitors.
- Due to an increase in arrivals, from 1992 to 1993 total earnings from tourism rose by F$35.5 million (K40.8 million), from F$328.1 million (K377.1 million) to F$363.6 million (K417.9 million).
- Tourism continued to be Fiji's largest contributor of foreign exchange earnings, accounting for around 62% of total domestic exports value in 1993. These earnings represented around 16.5% of GDP in 1993, accounting for an estimated direct employment of 14 000 people (about 15% of total paid employment) in that period.

A number of factors contributed to the increased tourist arrivals to Fiji over this period, such as increased marketing budgets and a greater number of flights.

These facts demonstrate that tourism is an important sector in Fiji's national economy.

Traditional-style villas and resorts draw huge numbers of tourists to Fiji every year. What might be the costs and benefits of having a specially built resort for tourists?

Unit 11.3 Activity 2A: Tourism in Fiji – short-answer questions

1. What advantages does Fiji have as a tourist destination?
2. What factors could cause a downturn in tourism in Fiji?
3. Compare and contrast tourism in Fiji to tourism in PNG. What strategies can you suggest for improving PNG's tourism profile?

Tourism in Vanuatu: a case study

Vanuatu is part of Oceania and is an island group in the South Pacific Ocean, about three-quarters of the way from Hawaii to Australia (16°S and 167°E). Its capital city is Port Vila, situated on the island of Efate. Formerly called the New Hebrides, Vanuatu experienced both British and French colonisation, changing its name to Vanuatu when it gained independence in 1980. It is a republic with a parliamentary system of government.

Vanuatu has more than 80 islands, of which about 65 are inhabited. Its estimated population of 227 574 is made up of Ni-Vanuatu (Vanuatu citizens, 98.5%) and others (1.5%) according to the 1999 census. With a land area of 12 189 square kilometres and a coastline of 2528 kilometres, it has a population density of 18 persons per square kilometre and in 2011 its estimated GDP per capita was US$4900 (K10 481). The economy is supported by tourism, small-scale agriculture, fishing and offshore financial services. Several religious denominations practise in Vanuatu. Vanuatu is also a member of SPTO.

Vanuatu stretches from the Banks and Torres islands in the north to the islands of Tanna and Aneityum in the south. Vanuatu offers 946 tourist rooms, with most facilities on the main island, Efate. Activity also occurs on Tanna (the location of the active Yasur volcano), Espiritu Santo and Pentecost (renowned for the ritual of N'gol, a traditional forerunner of bungee jumping in which young people jump from a tree, attached by vine leaves around their ankles). The lure of Vanuatu is in resort tourism based on beach and water activities, although business tourism (including conferences and incentives) accounts for a fifth of tourist arrivals. Vanuatu is also developing a reputation for cruise tourism (mainly to Efate but also to Luganville on Espiritu Santo and to Tanna), and diving (mainly on Espiritu Santo, the site for wreck diving on the *President Coolidge*). Vanuatu retains its diverse cultures; its traditional *kastom* (customs) include extensive taboos but represent a resource of potential interest for tourist markets.

Economic development in Vanuatu is hindered by dependence on relatively few commodity exports, vulnerability to natural disasters, and long distances from the main markets and between constituent islands. In mid-2002 the government stepped up efforts to boost tourism, through improved air connections, resort development and cruise-ship facilities. Agriculture, especially livestock farming, is a second area targeted for growth. Australia and New Zealand are the main sources of tourists and foreign aid.

There are opportunities for investment in the following sub-sectors:

* Accommodation upgrading, extension and development – mainly for small boutique or eco-resorts.
* Marketing and technology partnerships – through website development and facility and infrastructure design.
* Inter-island cruising.
* Marine and diving operations.

Highlighted below are some brief facts about tourism in Vanuatu (as presented by the Vanuatu Tourism Office and TCSP and covering the period 1990 to 1997):

* Tourist arrivals increased in a four-year period from 42 140 in 1994 to 49 605 in 1997. The major source markets were Australia (28 973 or 58%), New Zealand (6109 or 12.3%), other Pacific (2993 or 6%), other Europe (2893) and other countries (1101).
* Purpose of visit in 1997 was as follows: pleasure and holiday (73%), business (13%) and VFR (6.9%).
* Seasonality of arrivals: observations suggest that the first half of the year is the low season while the second half is the high season.
* Average length of stay, measured by intended stay (in nights) declared on passenger arrival cards, was 8.4 nights.
* In 1997 there was a total of 48 hotel establishments offering 717 rooms, the majority located at Port Vila.
* In 1997 total tourism earnings were US$46 million (K98.4 million) from 49 605 arrivals, which provided employment for about 1300 people.

Other sectors that contribute to GDP (2011) include agriculture (21.2%) and industry (10.2%). But services contribute the majority (68.4%). Tourism is clearly the top foreign exchange earner for the country.

Traditional bungee jumping in Vanuatu. Adventure tourism is growing in popularity. What opportunities can you think of for developing adventure activities for tourists in PNG?

Cruise tourism has become a popular tourist attraction for Vanuatu. Research cruise tourism in PNG and assess its importance. What recommendations can you make for the development of cruise tourism in our country?

Unit 11.3 Activity 2B: Tourism in Vanuatu – short-answer questions

1. What advantages does Vanuatu have as a tourist destination?
2. What factors could cause a downturn in tourism in Vanuatu?
3. Compare and contrast tourism in Vanuatu to tourism in PNG. In what areas is PNG doing better or worse than Vanuatu?

Tourism in Cook Islands: a case study

Cook Islands is part of Oceania and is an island group in the South Pacific Ocean, about half way between Hawaii and New Zealand (21°14'S and 159°46'W). Its capital is Avarua, situated on the main island of Rarotonga. Formerly referred to as the Harvey Islands, it was named after Captain Cook who sighted the islands in 1770. The islands became a British protectorate in 1888 and by 1900 administrative control was transferred to New Zealand. In 1965 the citizens chose independent self-government, in free association with New Zealand. The system of government is a parliamentary democracy.

Fifteen islands and atolls make up Cook Islands, which are widely separated over two million square kilometres of the South Pacific Ocean. The total land area is 236 square kilometres with a coastline of 120 kilometres. The population of 10 777 people (2012 estimate) comprises Cook Island Maori (Polynesian, 87.7%), part Cook Island Maori (5.8%) and other (6.5%) according to the 2001 census. In 2005 GDP per capita was US$9100 (K19 465). In 2008, GDP composition by sector was agriculture (11.7%), industry (9.9%) and services (78.5%). Several religious denominations practise in Cook Islands. It is also a member of SPTO.

The sparsely populated islands in the north are mostly low coral atolls, proving attractive for adventurous travellers wanting to experience a remote island lifestyle. In the south are volcanic, hilly islands, providing different opportunities for tourists. Cook Islands offers all the coastal, marine and scenic attractions associated with tropical islands, plus a vibrant culture (manifested through island nights featuring traditional dancing) and good dining and entertainment facilities. Physically, the island of Rarotonga is dominated by high peaks with rain forests on the slopes, and is encircled by a reef enclosing a lagoon. This combination permits all water-based activities as well as safari tours, walks and climbs. Five other islands are all reached by a short flight from Rarotonga: Aitutaki is partly volcanic and partly of atoll origin; Atiu is a small island surrounded by a close reef and shallow lagoon, with numerous sandy coves and beaches, and rainforest on its raised volcanic centre; Mauke is the garden island; Mangaia has a rugged coastline with a lush green interior, its *makatea* (fossilised coral) containing a network of caves; and Mitiaro has two large freshwater lakes in its interior.

Tourism investment opportunities for Cook Islands fall into the categories of resort development, transport, cultural attractions and service support. These opportunities include:

* Development of a network of resorts in the Polynesian islands.
* Development of boutique and eco-oriented resorts.
* Culture-based tourist attractions (e.g. cultural centre, *vaka* – a traditional Polynesian canoe attraction).
* Accident and emergency centre.
* Inter-island transport (by helicopter, and by sea using a traditional Polynesian vessel).

Highlighted below are some facts about tourism in Cook Islands for the period 1990 to 1997 (as presented by the Cook Islands Tourism Corporation and TCSP):

* Tourist arrivals increased from 33 882 in 1990 to 49 964 in 1997. The major source markets were New Zealand followed by Europe, USA, Canada and Australia.
* Purpose of visit: The majority were for holidays (92%), with a small number of business arrivals (4.1%), VFR (0.3%) and other purpose (3.5%).

- Seasonality of arrivals: observations indicate that the first six months of the year are the slower months, with most activity in the second half of the year.
- Earnings from tourism totalled US$62 million (K132.6 million) in 1997. In 1993, total foreign exchange earnings from tourism were estimated at about US$31 million (K66.3 million). This represented an increase of about US$3 million (K6.4 million) over the previous year's earnings of US$27.2 million (K58.18 million). Cook Islands exported goods (mostly fruits and vegetables, pearls and some manufactured goods) worth only US$500 000 during the same period. Thus, tourism earnings were about 62 times higher than the value of total domestic exports. GDP value in 1993 (measured in current value cost prices) was US$84 million (K179.7 million). As a result, tourism earnings as a proportion of GDP were as high as 36.8%, directly employing an estimated 404 people. On this basis we can conclude that tourism is a dominant sector of economic activity in Cook Islands.

Like many other South Pacific island nations, economic development in Cook Islands is hampered by the country's distance from foreign markets, the limited size of the domestic market, a lack of natural resources, periodic devastation from natural disasters, and inadequate infrastructure. The emigration of skilled workers to New Zealand is a problem, although remittances from expatriates, together with foreign aid, help to offset trade deficits. The country lived beyond its means in the 1980s and 1990s but since 2000 the sale of state assets, a strengthening of economic management, the encouragement of tourism, and a debt-restructuring agreement have all stimulated investment and growth. Tourism plays an important role in earning foreign exchange and in alleviating balance-of-payment problems.

Places such as the Mangaia caves, which are famous burial caves in Cook Islands, are unusual attractions. Research similar places in PNG that could become tourist attractions. What might be the advantages and the disadvantages for local people?

Aitutaki Lagoon, one of the many tourist attractions in Cook Islands. Research some places in PNG that would compare with a lagoon like this.

Unit 11.3 Activity 2C: Tourism in Cook Islands – short-answer questions

1. What advantages does Cook Islands have as a tourist destination?
2. What factors could cause a downturn in tourism in Cook Islands?
3. Compare some of the statistics given for Cook Islands with statistical information gathered on PNG. What can you generally comment on?

Unit 11.4 Tourism Information
Topic 1: Information for the tourist

Tourism information is vital for tourists and the development of the industry. Unit 11.4 introduces students to the various sources and types of tourism information and provides opportunities to develop skills and processes, assess the validity and value of information, and apply it in relevant situations. Students are expected to:

- Demonstrate an understanding of the importance of tourism at local, national, regional and international level.
- Identify the role of tourism in the economic growth of a country.
- Demonstrate an understanding of the impact of tourism at individual, local, national, regional and global levels.
- Communicate tourism information in a variety of ways and settings.

Introduction

People will always need information in order to make good decisions. A problem for tourists making travel arrangements, particularly at the last minute, is that they do not have the luxury of time. Although developments in ICT (information and communication technologies) have made it easier for potential tourists to access information quickly through the Internet or other technologies such as mobile phones, there remains the problem of information overload – large quantities of information that can confuse rather than assist a potential tourist in making the best travel decisions. Our aim should be to make the decision-making process easy and convenient for the potential traveller.

If we are to meet tourists' needs for information, we must understand the basis on which they make decisions. The diagram on page 72 sets out choices made by potential travellers when selecting destinations (and tourism products and services). This is done through a process of elimination that involves the following:

- Awareness set – destinations easily identified by potential travellers.
- Unaware set – destinations the traveller has no knowledge of or does not easily recall.
- Available set – initial set of feasible alternatives, i.e. initially those destinations with available information that can be considered.
- Unavailable set – extravagantly difficult destinations are rejected, such as those about which it is too difficult to access information.
- Early consideration set – possible destinations to visit soon, based on additional information that has been acquired.
- Inept set – destinations associated with unpleasant experiences.
- Inert set – destinations with neither positive nor negative associations (this could imply that little is known about the destination, or that it is considered uninteresting).
- Late consideration set – usually between two and five destinations are seriously considered, once additional information has been obtained and impractical destinations or those no longer thought desirable have been excluded.
- Inaction set – no further information available or sought on these destinations.

- Action set – highly active search process in order to make decision.
- Final rejected set – last one or two destinations to be rejected.
- Single choice destination – the decision is made in favour of one destination.

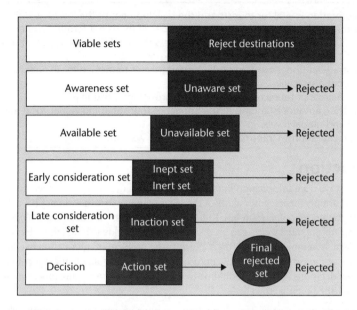

A comprehensive overview of choice set terms (source: Um & Crompton 1990)

The diagram opposite shows other factors that influence the information needs of potential travellers. The 'push' factors cause a potential tourist to leave their home (e.g. to escape boredom at home) and the 'pull' factors attract a potential tourist to a destination (e.g. warm weather or exotic cultures and scenery). These push and pull factors give rise to 'need recognition'. This means that a potential tourist realises that he or she could satisfy a need outside their home region, such as meeting a need to socialise, or gain social status by going on a holiday.

The subsequent search for information might begin with creating an overall image of the possible destination, which can lead to a tentative travel decision. After gathering additional information the image is refined; this might either confirm the original tentative decision or lead to a search for alternatives (which follows the same process).

This is not to suggest that *all* travel decisions follow this process; even after a choice has been made, people might still change their plans, based on additional information or simply through acting on 'gut feeling'.

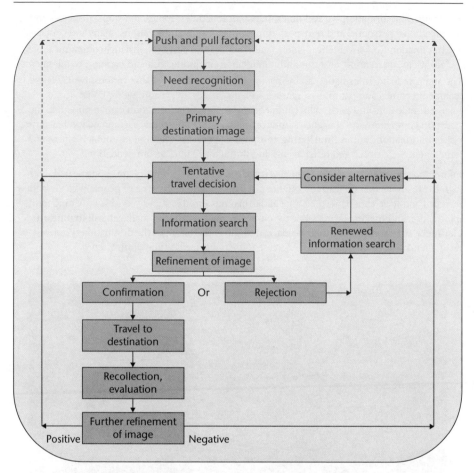

The destination decision process (source: Weaver & Oppermann 2000)

Tourists need information prior to travel, during travel and while they are at the destination. The information needs of tourists fall into four broad categories:

- Destination/product-specific information – specifically describes the destination, product or service and tries to promote and sell its benefits to potential tourists.
- Life concern information – protects the traveller's health and safety. This covers details of inoculations, insurance, bad weather and anything else that could cause serious discomfort or might be life-threatening. It might list places that are unsafe to visit and products or services that may be unsafe to experience; experiences unsuitable for certain types of people; allergies; level of disability access; non-smoking rules; appropriate behaviour and clothing.

- Logistical information – travel times, transport schedules, routes and stops, distances and directions, personnel and transport, tipping policy, sites and locations, maps and contacts.
- Information for convenience – information about local currency, driving, communications, electricity, quarantine, customs and immigration (including visa and passport requirements).

The aim is to make information accessible to potential tourists by using various media. These include brochures and pamphlets, newspapers, magazines, television, radio, DVDs, the Internet, trade fairs and personal recommendations. Tourist information can be presented by transport companies, travel agencies, tour operators and wholesalers, accommodation facilities, visitor information centres, **marketing companies**, government missions, branch offices and representatives, citizens and other agents and through personal recommendations.

Information must be factual and reliable. Travellers in the 21st century are sophisticated, with high expectations that their needs will be met. This is particularly true of people who are widely travelled and have experienced a range of destinations, products and services. Providing tourist information and making it accessible to tourists through a range of media and **distribution channels**, so that it satisfies their needs, can improve the image of the destination. Positive recommendations can improve and increase tourism business to the destination.

Global booking systems, also known as global distribution systems (GDS), are used by travel agents worldwide. They store and retrieve information related to air travel. For example, in addition to an airline booking, a computer reservation system such as Galileo can be used to book coach or train travel, cruises, car rental and hotel rooms, all linked to the airline booking.

Unit 11.4 Activity 1: Information for the tourist

1. For each tourist information need, identify the relevant information category:

Tourist information need	Information category
Insurance for personal valuables	
Universal Time Coordinates (UTC) or International Time Differences	
Specific information concerning a restaurant: food served, opening and closing times, location	
Tourist itinerary details	
Information on medical treatments for malaria and cholera	
Airline booking information	
Description of a coastal village tour	

2. Identify who would be responsible and what media would be used to present information needed by tourists in the following cases:

Information phase	Distributor	Media	Type of information
Before tourists travel			
During travel			
When tourists are at the destination			

Unit 11.4 Tourism Information
Topic 2: Information for the tourism industry

Having considered in the previous Topic the importance of information for the tourist, we now look at information required by the tourism industry and its various sectors.

Introduction

Information is broadly defined as a collection of facts or knowledge from which decisions can be made. It is vital for the destination tourism industry to maintain up-to-date local knowledge if it is to meet and satisfy visitor needs and expectations. Such knowledge and information might include the following:

- History (e.g. origins of the indigenous people, early European contact, war).
- Land and resources (e.g. geographical location information, climate, vegetation, natural resources).
- Population (e.g. people, religion, education).
- Government (e.g. system, different levels and functions).
- Economy (e.g. export commodities, **imports**, transport, communication).
- Tourism (e.g. natural, cultural and historical attractions, accommodations, restaurants, entertainment facilities, visitor information centres, modes of transportation, arts and crafts, souvenirs, tour operators, airports and seaports).
- Support (complementary) services (e.g. commercial banks, postal services, shopping marts, chemists and pharmacies, telecommunications including Internet cafes, fire, police, ambulance, security, power supply, hair and beauty salons).
- Law (e.g. relevant legislation, industry standards and practices, licensing, consumer protection, insurance, **liability**, **torts** and disclosures, operating times, employment, customs and immigration, contracts, negotiation, **commissions**, cultural norms and traditions, investment and incentives, legal structure of business, making complaints).
- Research and statistics (e.g. number of tourist arrivals, average spending per tourist, industry profitability, supply side, demand side, reasons for visit, sites visited, activities undertaken, ratings, length of stay, future predictions or forecasts).

It is also important to know who are the partners (sectors) within the tourism (travel and hospitality) industry that organise, plan for and bring tourists into the country, and provide goods and services to satisfy their needs and to benefit from them. The diagram below identifies sectors in a tourism industry such as transport (e.g. airlines), marketing specialists (e.g. travel agents), accommodations (e.g. hotels and guest houses), attractions (natural, cultural, historical and built, e.g. national parks, caves and festivals), tour operations (e.g. Niugini Natural Tours), coordination (e.g. PNGTPA and provincial tourism bureaus and information centres) and miscellaneous (e.g. souvenirs and arts and crafts). Many other industries and sectors are involved, such as security and police, recreational and sports facilities, retail businesses, banking, ICT and postal services. The identified sectors should also work together in a cooperative and coordinated way, so that tourism becomes a viable industry and benefits all.

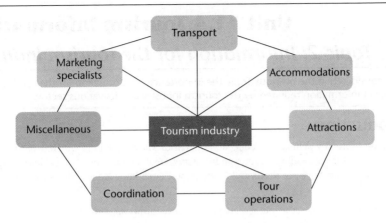

Sectors in a tourism industry

The tourism industry is predominantly service based. Characteristics of service are:

- Intangibility – Unlike physical products, a service cannot be physically examined ('search' qualities), checked ('experience' qualities) or tested ('credence' qualities). A service is the result of a deed, performance, effort or encounter in time. It ceases to exist at the moment it is rendered. For these reasons it can be difficult to know how to price and signal service quality. Possible solutions to this problem include creating strong brands, providing tangible (physical) evidence and offering service guarantees.

- Inseparability – In a service environment, production and consumption of service take place at the same time; in most hospitality services, both the service provider and the customer must be present for the transaction to occur. The customer specifying the order is involved in the production process, and the customer contact employee who takes down the order is also part of the product. Production and consumption cannot be entirely separated in time, which presents problems. One solution is to manage the customer's role in production, for example by asking the customer whether they would prefer a thin or thick base for the pizza they are ordering.

- Variability and heterogeneity – Service quality depends on who provides the service and when and where it is provided. Because once a service has been rendered it is in one sense 'gone', it can be difficult to maintain consistency in service quality output. One solution is to specify all activities and processes in detail, such as by standardisation. Examples of business that do this include fast food chains such as McDonald's and Big Rooster.

- Perishability – Services cannot be stored. This means that any opportunity or revenue lost is lost forever. Strategies to maximise the number of customers buying the service include queuing systems in shops (e.g. in a bank) and over-booking (e.g. in airlines).

It is also important to understand exactly what customers are buying or paying for. Theodore Levitt (1980) explained that every product or service that is marketed has four incarnations:

- Generic – what the customer is *really* paying for. For example, in a hotel, the customer is paying for the bed. The customer cannot be expected to pay for hotel accommodation and then sleep on the floor.

- Expected – all the traditional services that customers expect, such as convenient delivery, attractive terms and conditions, and clean room and sheets.

- Augmented – additions to the product, to make up a bundle of benefits. This may exceed customer satisfaction. For example, a chocolate on the pillow or tea- and coffee-making facilities in the hotel room.

- Potential – If the three incarnations above are not successful, the **supplier** must focus on everything that can be done to attract and hold customers and that can be added to the augmented product in future.

Suppliers of tourism products and services need to be able to identify and segment different customer groups, based on their specific needs and expectations. In this way suppliers can meet each customer's expectations and thus sustain their business. This is called market segmentation. The table below explains four major segmentation variables for consumer markets.

GEOGRAPHIC	
Region	E.g. Europe, the Americas (North and South), Asia, the Pacific, Africa.
DEMOGRAPHIC	
Age	E.g. under 6 years, 6–11, 12–19, etc.
Family size	E.g. 1–2 family members, 3–4 members, more than 5.
Family life cycle	E.g. bachelor (young and single, likes fun and excitement); newly married; full nest 1 (planning and preparing for children); full nest 2 (have older children who are unlikely to accompany their parents on vacation); empty nest (later adulthood, more discretionary income and time); solitary survivors (widowed travellers); DINKS (double income with no kids, both members of couple earning).
Gender	Male, female.
Income	Under K5000; K5000–10 999; K11 000–15 999; K16 000–20 999; K21 000–25 999; K26 000–30 999; K31 000 or over.
Occupation	E.g. professional and technical, manager, official, business proprietor, clerical, sales.
Education	Elementary school; primary/community school; high school; national high/secondary/matriculation; college – undergraduate or postgraduate.
Religion	Catholic, Protestant, Jewish, Muslim, Hindu, other.
Race	White, black, Asian.
Generation	Baby boomers (people born between the end of World War II (1945) and the early 1960s, when certain economies and the birth rate – particularly in the US – were booming); Generation X (people born from the mid-1960s to the 1970s – tend to be more cynical); Generation Y (people born in the 1980s and 1990s – very sophisticated in evaluating products and services).
Nationality	Japanese, Australian, New Zealander.
Social class	Lower class, middle class, upper class.
PSYCHOGRAPHIC	
Lifestyle	Straights, swingers, long-hairs.
Personality	Compulsive, gregarious, authoritarian, ambitious.

BEHAVIOURAL	
Occasion	Regular occasion, special occasion.
Benefits	Quality, service, economy, speed.
User status	Non-user, ex-user, potential user, first-time user, regular user.
Usage rate	Light user, medium user, heavy user.
Loyalty status	None, medium, strong, absolute.
Buyer-readiness stage	Unaware, aware, informed, interested, desirous, intending to buy.
Attitude toward product	**Enthusiastic**, positive, indifferent, negative, hostile.

Major segmentation variables for consumer markets (source: Kotler 1997)

The PNG Tourism Promotion Authority, in compiling visitor survey reports, uses some of these segmentation criteria when analysing purpose of visit, activities undertaken, places visited, travel companion and visitor expenditure. It is important for suppliers to learn about these market segments by researching trends and asking questions about their potential profitability, such as the number of existing competitors catering to each segment; current profits of companies operating in the segment; costs involved in entering the segment; the size and growth rate of the segment; relative ease or difficulty of communicating with the segment; price and demand elasticity; threat of unemployment; the susceptibility of **exchange rate** fluctuations on the price of the product for each segment; and the ease of packaging the product for each segment (e.g. bundling accommodation and flights).

*Serving customers is an important aspect of the tourism industry. Discuss the meaning of service and give examples of good **customer service** in hotels, restaurants and shops.*

Discuss the importance of rental cars in destination tourism. Research the car rental options in a major town near you and compare the costs of the different car rental firms.

Unit 11.4 Activity 2: Information for the tourism industry – short-answer questions

1. How can you make tangible a service that is intangible in the following cases:
   a. Restaurant service.
   b. Hotel accommodation.
   c. Sightseeing village scenery.
   d. Tour guiding.

2. Identify the four service incarnations in the following cases:
   a. Ordering a meat-lover pizza.
   b. Making a booking for a Fifth-Element hire car.
   c. Trekking Mt Wilhelm.

Unit 11.4 Tourism Information
Topic 3: How information is delivered

Having looked at the information needs of tourists and those involved in the tourism industry, Topic 3 examines how tourism information is delivered.

Introduction

In trying to communicate relevant information to potential clients, suppliers of tourism products and services need to understand the **travel distribution process**.

An inbound tour operator (ITO) such as Trans Niugini Tours puts together a local PNG program by combining products and services from a range of principals or service providers – such as accommodations in hotels, seats in airlines, sightseeing and sing-sings in villages – under one packaged price, which includes the ITO's markup. The operator sells the program to an overseas tour wholesaler, who includes it in its overall package. This package also includes other destinations, products and services in other countries, transportation, the wholesaler's markup and retail travel agent's commission. The wholesaler sells the package to a retail travel agent who sells it to the final customer – the traveller.

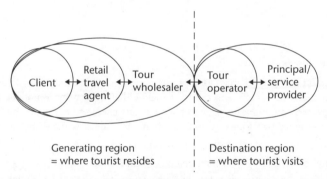

Travel distribution system

The retail travel agent, tour wholesaler and tour operator do not usually own what they sell (the components of the **tour package**); they are simply intermediaries or agents acting on behalf of the principals and service providers, earning commissions on what they sell. The final customer who pays for the package does not enter into a contract with these agents but with the principals and service providers, although in some cases agents can be held liable for providing false or misleading information.

There is a reverse payment relationship: the money that the travel agent collects does not belong to it. Rather, the travel agent must pay the wholesaler less its commission and the process is repeated along the chain until the principals and service providers are paid. In theory, the cost benefit of buying in bulk is passed on to the final customer.

The travel-buying process does not always have to follow this sequence. With the advent of new technologies, particularly the Internet, potential tourists can buy directly from principals, thereby cutting out the middleman.

Marketing is the means by which essential information concerning the destination products and services and their benefits are conveyed to potential tourists, using various forms of communication tools or media. The 'Four Ps' of the marketing mix (illustrated right) are **P**roduct, **P**rice, **P**romotion and **P**lace (distribution). These can be combined to communicate essential information to tourists and other visitors. Each of the Four Ps is explained below.

The Four Ps of the marketing mix

Product – refers to both physical products and services that serve as attractions for tourists; products are the reason why tourists decide to visit the destination. Without these there would be no point to tourism. Product is the total experience and not just one aspect. A few points to clarify:

- Products need to be correctly positioned in the market to attract customers; their benefits should suit the selected market segment.
- Products should be modified over time to meet changing needs.
- New products should be introduced to maintain customer interest and **enthusiasm**.
- Outdated or failing products should be withdrawn from the market.

Information about the product will also include:

- Product features (attributes).
- Brand identity (image).
- Packaging and labelling the product as a bundle of benefits.
- Provision of support services.

Price – the amount of money charged for a product or service; can also be defined as the sum of the values that consumers exchange for the benefit of having or using a product or service. In pricing, providers communicate value to potential customers and to their own organisation. Price can be determined by taking into consideration one or more of the following factors:

- Cost-based pricing – adding a reasonable markup to the cost of production.
- Competition-based pricing – trying to match or beat competitors' prices.
- Value-based pricing – a market-researched evaluation of customers' perceptions of value.
- Premium pricing – charging a high price for a luxury item because it has a unique quality, e.g. a luxury cruise or hotel room.
- Penetration pricing – a price set artificially low in order to gain market share. This is often used to bring a new product onto the market.
- Economy pricing – a no-frills, low price. Organisations keep marketing and manufacturing costs low so that they can charge the minimum price possible.
- Price skimming – Suppliers do this when they have an innovative product in the market. They charge a high price for customers who are eager and want to be the first to experience this product or service. The supplier can collect maximum revenue at this stage, and when competitors enter the market they drop this strategy.
- Trial-and-error assessment of the maximum that the market will bear.

Prices might be set to accommodate different types of clients or bookings, volume sales, exchange-rate fluctuations and seasonal factors. Also, a supplier might wish to charge a comfortable price that is not embarrassing to ask.

Promotion – organisations must communicate their offerings to customers. A promotion should grab **A**ttention, excite **I**nterest, create **D**esire and prompt **A**ction – **AIDA**. It should create a strong image, and reach, inform or remind and persuade the selected segment to react. An organisation's communications mix consists of the following elements:

- Advertising – any paid form of non-personal presentation and promotion of ideas, goods or services by an identified sponsor.
- Personal selling – agents or representatives of the organisation talking up the organsation in an effort to promote and sell the benefits to clients.
- Sales promotion – short-term incentives to encourage the purchase of a product or service, e.g. give-away product samples.
- Public relations – building good relations with the organisation's various publics by obtaining favourable publicity, building up a good corporate image and handling unfavourable rumours, e.g. getting the *Post-Courier* to publish an article about the opening of a new guest house or a forthcoming cultural festival.

The wide choice of media tools available for use in promotional activities includes newspapers, television, direct mail, radio, magazines, brochures, billboards, pop-ups on the Internet, movies, bus stops, public elevators, rest rooms, public transport, speeches, special events, annual reports, corporate identity materials and **community service** activities.

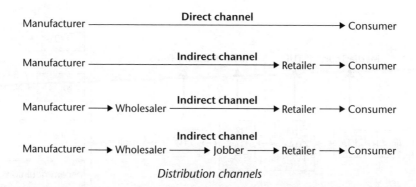

Distribution channels

Place (distribution) – The challenge is to make the product available to the target market. The diagram above shows different channels of distribution. The cost to the consumer and manufacturer in terms of the number of contacts between manufacturer and consumer is displayed in the diagram at the top of page 86. In case *A* (without a distributor), a potential tourist in Salzburg, Austria, who wants to visit Balek Wildlife Sanctuary in Madang and also needs transportation and accommodation, will have to contact the individual suppliers to confirm bookings and payments. This increases the number of contacts between the individual suppliers and the client and increases communication costs. But when a distributor is involved as in case *B*, the Austrian client only needs to visit Media Tours in Salzburg to pay for a tour package that contains all other components; this relationship is depicted in the diagram at the bottom of page 86, showing the **travel distribution system**.

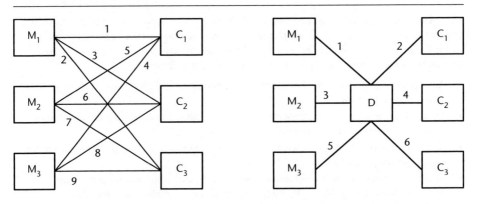

A Number of contacts without a distributor
$M \times C = 3 \times 3 = 9$

B Number of contacts with a distributor
$M + C = 3 + 3 = 6$

M = Manufacturer   C = Consumer   D = Distributor

Number of contacts between manufacturer and consumer
(source: Kotler, Bowen & Makens 2003)

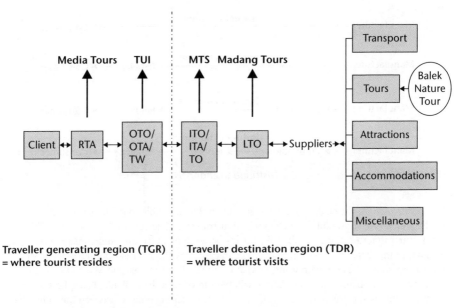

Traveller generating region (TGR)
= where tourist resides

Traveller destination region (TDR)
= where tourist visits

RTA = retail travel agent
OTO/OTA/TW = outbound tour operator/outgoing travel agent/tour wholesaler
ITO/ITA/TO = inbound tour operator/incoming travel agent/tour operator
LTO = local tour operator

Travel distribution system showing various suppliers

The basic questions arising from the Four Ps are as follows:

• What goods and services are being provided to satisfy customer needs and wants?
• For what price will these goods and services be sold, and at what cost to the customer?
• How will the target markets be informed and persuaded through effective communication?
• How will distribution take place in a way that is convenient for the customer?

These considerations should guide destinations and suppliers of tourism products and services to communicate their benefits effectively to clients, both locally and internationally.

*PNG's foreign missions, **destination management organisations,** and local and inbound tour operators promote and market PNG. They do this by making available relevant information so that potential tourists can easily arrange their trips to PNG. What skills would be important for these people?*

What can be done to inform tourists staying at a place like this about local tourism products and services?

Unit 11.4 Activity 3A: Delivery of tourism information

1. Fill in the table below by matching the descriptions with appropriate terms from the travel distribution system. The first example has been done for you.

Kokopo Tours	Local tour operator (LTO) – arranges tours in East New Britain Province. It becomes an inbound tour operator (ITO) if it also brings in clients from overseas and arranges tours to other parts of PNG.
Masurina Lodge	
Travel Air	
Kupunung Ku Kipe Cultural Centre	
Travcoa Luxury Travel in the USA	
PNG Holidays in Australia	
Air Niugini Travel Service in Australia	
Touristik Union International (TUI) in Germany	
Kokoda Trek	
Hertz Rent-a-Car	

2. Describe how you would combine the Four *P*s to communicate to clients the benefits of some products or services that you know.

Unit 11.4 Activity 3B: Analysing a case study – advertising choices

A lodge in town spends K8000 a year on marketing through various media, in the following order of priority:

- Newspaper.
- *Yellow Pages*.
- Leaflet drop.
- Special events.
- Community service.

The lodge then conducts a 'How did you find us?' survey of its customers. This reveals:

- 38% were existing customers.
- 28% were referrals.
- 12% read the newspaper.

- 8% came through the *Yellow Pages*.
- 6% came from the leaflet drop.
- 5% came through the special events.
- 3% came through public service.

How do you think the business would react to this? Prepare a proposal for the lodge, outlining how you would allocate its marketing budget.

Unit 12.1 Global Tourism

Topic 1: Introduction

Tourism is a global phenomenon. It is one of the world's largest industries, creating jobs across national and international economies. It can create prosperity and sustainable development and rescue people from poverty. This Unit looks at the world's major geographical features, in both established and emerging tourism-generating regions. Students are expected to:

- Demonstrate an understanding of the importance of tourism at local, national, regional and international levels.
- Describe and explain the growth of local, national, regional and global tourism.
- Demonstrate an understanding of the impact of tourism at individual, local, national, regional and global levels.
- Communicate tourism information in a variety of ways and settings.

The World Travel and Tourism Council (WTTC, based in Brussels, Belgium) is an authority on the global economic and social contributions of travel and tourism. At the time of writing this book, the WTTC stated that the travel and tourism industry was expected to grow by 2.8 per cent in 2012, marginally faster than the global rate of economic growth, which was predicted to be 2.5 per cent. This rate of growth meant that the travel and tourism industry was expected to directly contribute US$2 trillion (K4.2 trillion) to the global economy and sustain some 100.3 million jobs (WTTC 7 March 2012).

The table below, produced by UNWTO, shows world tourism rankings in 2010.

World's top ten international tourism destinations in 2010, out of a global total of 940 million tourists		
Rank	Country	International tourist arrivals
1	France	76.80 million
2	United States	59.75 million
3	China	55.67 million
4	Spain	52.68 million
5	Italy	43.63 million
6	United Kingdom	28.13 million
7	Turkey	27.00 million
8	Germany	26.88 million

9	Malaysia	24.58 million
10	Mexico	22.40 million
Top ten destinations in Africa in 2010, out of a total of over 49 million tourists		
1	Morocco	9.29 million
2	South Africa	8.07 million
3	Tunisia	6.90 million
4	Zimbabwe	2.24 million
5	Mozambique	(2009) 2.22 million
6	Algeria	(2009) 1.91 million
7	Botswana	(2009) 1.55 million
8	Nigeria	(2009) 1.41 million
9	Kenya	(2009) 1.39 million
10	Namibia	(2009) 0.98 million
Top ten destinations in the Middle East in 2010, out of a total of almost 60 million tourists		
1	Egypt	14.05 million
2	Saudi Arabia	10.85 million
3	Syria	8.55 million
4	United Arab Emirates	7.43 million
5	Bahrain	(2007) 4.94 million
6	Jordan	4.56 million
7	Israel	3.50 million
8	Lebanon	2.17 million
9	Qatar	(2009) 1.66 million
10	Oman	(2009) 1.52 million

Top ten destinations in the Americas in 2010, out of a total of almost 150 million tourists	
1 United States	59.75 million
2 Mexico	22.40 million
3 Canada	16.10 million
4 Argentina	5.29 million
5 Brazil	6.16 million
6 Dominican Republic	4.13 million
7 Puerto Rico	3.68 million
8 Chile	2.77 million
9 Cuba	2.51 million
10 Colombia	2.39 million
Top ten destinations in Asia and the Pacific in 2010, out of a total of almost 204 million tourists	
1 China	55.67 million
2 Malaysia	24.58 million
3 Hong Kong	20.09 million
4 Thailand	15.84 million
5 Macau	11.93 million
6 Singapore	9.16 million
7 South Korea	8.80 million
8 Japan	8.61 million
9 Indonesia	7.00 million
10 Australia	5.89 million

Top ten destinations in Europe in 2010, out of a total of almost 477 million tourists	
1 France	76.70 million
2 Spain	52.68 million
3 Italy	43.63 million
4 United Kingdom	28.13 million
5 Turkey	27.00 million
6 Germany	26.88 million
7 Austria	22.00 million
8 Ukraine	21.20 million
9 Russia	20.27 million
10 Greece	15.01 million

International tourist arrivals by country of destination, 2010
(sources: Wikipedia & UNWTO)

Based on the 2010 figures in the table above, the ranking by world region in descending order is as follows: Europe (477 million tourist arrivals); Asia-Pacific (204 million); Americas (150 million); Middle East (60 million) and Africa (49 million). It should be noted that the distribution and share of tourist numbers and receipts (earnings from tourism) are uneven in individual countries and territories. This is also true of destinations not listed here. Of course the picture of world tourism rankings presented above will have changed while this book was in preparation.

In 2012 the UNWTO (16 January 2012) reported that international tourist arrivals grew by 4.4% in 2011, to a total of 980 million, up from 939 million in 2010. This occurred in a year characterised by stalled global economic recovery, major political changes in the Middle East and North Africa and natural disasters in Japan. Europe maintained its lead position in 2011 with 6% growth, with tourist arrivals reaching 503 million in 2011, accounting for 28 million of the 41 million additional international arrivals recorded worldwide. The Americas (4% growth) saw an increase of 6 million arrivals, reaching 156 million in total. Africa maintained international arrivals at 50 million, as the gain of 2 million (+7%) by sub-Saharan destinations was offset by the losses in North Africa (–12%). The Middle East lost an estimated 5 million (–8%) of its international tourist arrivals, down to 55 million. Nevertheless, some destinations such as Saudi Arabia, Oman and the United Arab Emirates sustained steady growth.

Asia and the Pacific was up by 11 million arrivals (+6%) in 2011, reaching a total of 216 million international tourists. South Asia and South-East Asia both increased by 9%, benefiting from strong intraregional demand, while growth was comparatively weaker in North-East Asia (+4%) and Oceania (+0.3%), due partly to the temporary decline in the Japanese outbound market.

Available data on international **tourism receipts** and expenditure for 2011 closely followed the positive trend in arrivals. Among the top ten tourist destinations, receipts were up significantly in the USA (+12%), Spain (+9%), Hong Kong (+25%) and the UK (+7%).

The biggest increase in spending in 2011 was led by these countries' source markets among the emerging economies: China (+38%), Brazil (+32%), India (+32%) and Russia (+21%). These were followed by traditional markets, with the growth in expenditure of travellers from Germany (+4%) and the USA (+5%) above the levels of the previous year.

UNWTO forecast positive growth in international tourism in 2012, although at a slower rate. Arrivals were expected to increase by 3% to 4%, reaching the historic one billion mark by the end of 2012. The UNWTO predicated that emerging economies would regain the lead as a result of stronger growth in Asia and the Pacific and Africa (+4% to 6%), followed by the Americas and Europe (+2% to 4%). It also predicted that the Middle East would recover part of its losses from 2011 (between 0% and 5% growth).

When its wider economic effects are taken into account, the travel and tourism industry is forecast to contribute some US$6.5 trillion (K13.8 trillion) to the global economy and generate 260 million jobs – or 1 in 12 of all jobs on the planet, according to the WTTC. Based on the same source, in 2011 travel and tourism's total economic contribution, taking account its direct, indirect and induced impacts, was US$6.3 trillion (K13.4 trillion) in GDP; 255 million jobs; US$743 billion (K1580.85 billion) in investment; and US$1.2 trillion (K2.5 trillion) in exports. This contribution represented 9% of world GDP, 1 in 12 jobs, 5% of investment and 5% of exports.

David Scowsill, President and CEO of the WTTC, has stated: 'It is clear that the Travel and Tourism industry is going to be a significant driver of global growth and employment for the next decade. Our industry is responsible for creating jobs, pulling people out of poverty, and broadening horizons. It is one of the world's great industries'. Below are some highlights from research conducted by the WTTC and reported at the time of writing:

- South Asia and North-East Asia will be the fastest-growing regions in 2012, growing by 6.7%. This will be driven by countries such as India and China, where rising incomes will generate an increase in domestic tourism spend and a sharp upturn in capital investment, and by recovery in Japan.
- After an extremely challenging 2011, when civil unrest and violence had a dramatic effect on demand for Egypt, Tunisia and Libya, North Africa is showing signs of recovery in 2012 with travel and tourism direct GDP growth forecast at 3.6%. Morocco (8.3% forecast growth) will be the star performer of this region while negative perceptions of security continue to affect tourism in Egypt and Tunisia.
- In the Middle East, where civil unrest and violence continue in some countries, growth will be more subdued (3%), although there are stark differences between individual nations. Qatar will grow fastest at 13.2%, while Syria will likely see another dramatic fall, estimated at 20.5%, as the political situation worsens, increasing concerns over security. It is worth noting that 14% of all international arrivals in the Middle East in 2010 were in Syria, the third most important destination in the region after Egypt and Saudi Arabia, but civil unrest since then has devastated Syria's tourism industry.

- The mature economies of North America and Europe will continue to struggle in 2012. North America, which saw a slight upturn in the USA's economic situation at the end of 2011, should see growth of only 1.3% in travel and tourism direct GDP over the year.
- The prospects for travel and tourism growth in Europe in 2012 are precarious. Current forecasts suggest a 0.3% increase in travel and tourism direct GDP for the region over all, but this will be propped up by newer economies such as Poland and by Russia. A decline of 0.3% is expected across the European Union. Consumer spending is set to tighten as austerity measures kick in, and there continues to be considerable uncertainty around the future of the Eurozone and the economies of Greece, Spain, Italy and Portugal.

The United Nations World Tourism Organization (UNWTO) is the international umbrella organisation responsible for the promotion of tourism interests at the global level. What are the advantages of having such an organisation? What disadvantages might there be?

Unit 12.1 Activity 1: World tourism – short-answer questions

1. Would you say that the international tourist arrival figures have changed now compared to 2010 figures? What are your reasons?

2. What does this mean for intraregional travel? (E.g. in 2011, arrivals in both South Asia and South-East Asia increased by 9%, as a result of strong intraregional demand.)

3. UNWTO predicted positive growth for the Asia-Pacific region (4–6% increase) in 2012. Does this mean all individual destinations within the region will experience the same level of growth? What are your reasons?

Unit 12.1 Global Tourism
Topic 2: Major geographical features of tourist regions

Following the introduction to global tourism presented in Topic 1, we now look at the geographical features of established and emerging tourist regions.

Established regions include Europe, North America, Australia, New Zealand and Pacific Islands such as Fiji. Emerging tourist regions include Asia, South America, Russia, eastern Europe and Papua New Guinea.

Geography is a wide-ranging discipline; its relevance to tourism lies in the spatial aspects of tourism. The geographer's approach sheds light on the following:

- The location of tourist areas.
- The movement of people, caused by tourism locales.
- Changes that tourism facilities bring to the landscape.
- The dispersion of tourism development.
- Physical planning.
- Economic, social and cultural problems.

To understand the geography of tourism, we begin with a model of a basic whole-tourism system, illustrated in the diagram below.

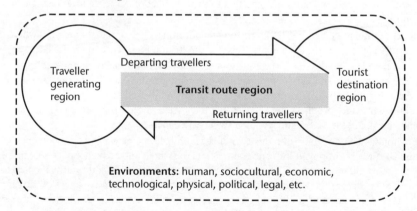

Location of travellers – tourists and of the travel and tourism industry

A basic whole-tourism system (source: Leiper 1995)

Tourists set out on a trip from where they live, identified here as a traveller-generating region (TGR). These departing travellers move through a transit route region (TRR), using various transportation modes, before reaching a tourist destination region (TDR). The reverse process occurs on their return journey. The tourist destination region is the place on a tourist's itinerary where he or she wants to spend time, and contains tourism resources that are of interest to the tourist.

Tourism occurs in an environment and has human consequences: sociocultural, economic, environmental and others. For example, when potential travellers in a TGR decide to travel to a destination for a holiday, they visit a nearby travel agent to make bookings and pay for a travel package. While in transit, individual travellers may buy duty-free items on the plane or shop at a convenience store in an airport, thus bringing economic consequences. While tourists are staying at their destination, they interact with local people and buy local artefacts; this has both sociocultural and economic consequences. Due to global concerns for the protection and enhancement of the natural environment, airlines are obliged to use the latest technologies in **energy efficiency**, while travellers try to avoid polluting or overcrowding ecologically sensitive areas. These activities and decisions have technological and environmental consequences.

The six essential elements or components of a whole-tourism system as illustrated on the previous page are as follows:

- Tourist – the human element: a person who travels from the TGR to the TDR via a TRR experiences the tourism products and services, and returns home via a TRR. It is because of this human element that we have a tourism industry.

- Traveller-generating region (TGR) – where the tourist normally resides. Certain conditions in a TGR might enable or encourage the tourist to set out on a trip, such as more holidays, more leisure time, economic power, boredom or unpleasant weather.

- Transit region (TR) – The places the tourist visits or passes through, and the transportation used, while travelling to reach the destination, and again on the return journey. TRs serve a useful purpose on a tourist's itinerary; they allow passengers to catch their breath and connect to smooth onward transportation to their destination, or to their residence when returning home.

- Tourist destination region (TDR) – the original idea (place) on a tourist's itinerary where the tourist wants to spend time to experience the destination products and services.

- Transportation and the travel and tourism industry – Without transportation and the travel and tourism industry, it is difficult to imagine tourism existing now, or in the future. Transportation moves the tourist to the destination and back. The travel and tourism industry provides products and services that the traveller needs in order to enhance their enjoyment and satisfaction during their travel experiences.

- Environments – The tourism industry influences and affects the general environment. Similarly, the environment influences and affects the whole tourism experience. For instance, if the transportation sector – which brings tourists to a destination and returns them to their place of residence – is permitted to operate without care for the consequences of the gases it emits, we can expect a build-up of greenhouse gases in the atmosphere, which could lead to global warming. The rise in the Earth's surface temperature could trigger changes in global weather patterns that affect sea levels and local climatic conditions. This can cause problems for travellers, e.g. a severe storm warning can delay flights and sea voyages, or cancellations of trips to destinations already booked. This may lead to further consequences such as loss of revenue and the need to deal with unhappy clients.

It is important to understand that all these different elements (components) are interrelated. Something affecting one element can affect another element. If potential travellers in a TGR do not earn much money in a particular year, not many of them can be expected to travel, which will reduce the profits earned by the travel and tourism industry and by destination providers. If uncontrolled tourist numbers visit an ecologically sensitive site, this will reduce the quality of the tourism resource; it will lose some of its attractiveness to future visitors, resulting in loss of reputation and revenue.

There may be several destinations and routes on a tourist's itinerary. This is explained in the diagram below:

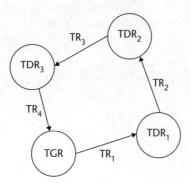

Geographical elements in a whole-tourism system with three destinations
(source: Leiper 1995)

The diagram above shows that a tourist has visited three different destinations (TDR_1, TDR_2 and TDR_3) and has moved through four different transit routes (TR_1, TR_2, TR_3 and TR_4) to make the journey out from and back to the TGR. This might be, for example, a tourist setting out on a trip from Germany spending two days in Singapore enjoying the city life, then travelling to PNG and spending five days enjoying the natural and cultural attractions in the country. The tourist then travels to Fiji to spend four days enjoying the culture and beaches of Fiji, before travelling to Australia to spend two days seeking out the desert environment, then flying out of Australia to get home to Germany. The different TDRs and TRs, use of transportation, and activities undertaken throughout the trip have consequences similar to those of the whole-tourism system.

Tourism destinations are not just destinations (places); they can be attractions, activities or ideas that provide tourism experiences and consequences. There are people living in each destination, with their daily lifestyles; they have expectations, and will experience the consequences of tourism. It is important to understand the interrelationships between the different components and how they function, in order to ensure the efficient and effective operation of the tourism industry. This can bring positive outcomes to all.

Describe the role that transit routes play in a whole-tourism system. What facilities might be provided for in-transit tourists to ensure they enjoy the break in their journey? Assess the role of Jackson's International Airport, Port Moresby, as a transit destination.

Unit 12.1 Activity 2: Geographical features of tourist regions – short-answer questions

1. Identify local conditions in a TGR that would enable a tourist to set out on a trip.

2. Identify services and providers on transit routes that would be useful to tourists.

3. Describe different consequences (political, economic, sociocultural, environmental) on the general environment, caused by tourists interacting with the destination.

4. Think of an example of a tourist itinerary (travel plan) and recreate the diagram 'Geographical elements in a whole-tourism system with three destinations'. Label your diagram based on descriptions from your itinerary.

Unit 12.1 Global Tourism
Topic 3: Characteristics of tourist regions

Tourism regions can play many different roles. In Topic 3 we consider some of the characteristics of these regions. The Topic concludes with a case study of educational tourism in PNG.

A tourism region can play multiple roles. It can serve as a TDR for incoming tourists, as a TR for tourists passing through, and its own residents might also participate in international tourism by taking outbound trips. Thus the TDR also acts as a TGR. Many countries with well-developed infrastructure, especially those with highly developed transport networks and infrastructure, could be described this way.

Almost all host government agencies that keep records of tourism activity report on tourist arrival numbers, destinations (sights and places) visited, and other activities undertaken by tourists.

But relatively little attention is paid to destinations acting as TRs and/or TGRs. The usefulness of such information is understood by the business community, as some local businesses target TR passengers while others target TDR passengers. For example, in various places in PNG there are local businesses that have flourished because of transit passengers. In Madang Town, two such places are Redscar along Modilon Road and LBC in the Newtown residential area. Redscar used to be a stopover point for buses carrying betel nut buyers from the Highlands. While at this transit point, the buyers would establish local contacts and transact other business, before setting off to Base Camp – past the north coast of Madang – to buy betel nut. They would then travel back to the Highlands by the same route. More recently, the bus stop was relocated from Redscar to LBC; the LBC area now performs this role. A simple trade store that operated in that area has greater customer numbers and has constructed an adjacent guest house to cater for the growing demand from transit passengers. This is a result of domestic tourism, under the guise of the informal sector.

Another benefit is experienced by governments when they negotiate international politics and trade. Many Papua New Guineans travel across the land border to Indonesia for leisure purposes and to conduct business. This exchange reinforces our relationship with Indonesia.

In a tourism system, traveller destinations include places along the way (TRs), places where travellers choose to stay a while (TDRs) and, finally, the end point of a tourist's journey: home (TGR). Although we might argue that any place where a tourist spends a night is as TDR, this is unnecessarily complicated. In the case of PNG therefore we define a TDR as the provincial capital in each province. Geographically large countries such as Australia and PNG can have many TDRs, while in a small country like Singapore a visitor can easily reach any place on a day trip.

At this point it is worth understanding the destination (tourist area) life cycle:

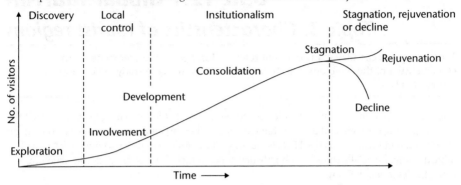

The tourist area life cycle (source: Butler 1980)

A tourist area, just like a person, goes through a life cycle. Its stages are described below:

- Exploration – A small number of adventurous tourists arrive; the main attractions are unspoilt natural or cultural features.
- Involvement – Local initiatives provide facilities and some advertising ensues; larger numbers of visitors arrive; a tourist season and **public sector** investment follow.
- Development – Large numbers of tourists arrive; control passes from locals to national or international companies; destination begins to change in appearance; overuse may begin.
- Consolidation – The destination is now a fully-fledged part of the tourism industry; the rate of increase in visitors is slowing; a recognisable recreational business district has emerged.
- Stagnation – Peak visitor numbers have been reached; the destination has become unfashionable; it has environmental, social or economic problems; major promotional efforts are needed to maintain visitor numbers.
- Decline – Visitors now visit newer, rural resorts as the destination goes into decline; it is dependent on a smaller geographical catchment and repeat visits.
- Rejuvenation – Authorities attempt to re-launch the destination by providing new facilities, attracting new markets and reinvesting.

This model can be applied to destination management and planning. It demonstrates how tourist destinations may evolve and what activities may be required at each stage to ensure sustainability. What are the features and conditions that shape evolution, making a destination popular? Several can be identified:

- Attractions – the major drawcards for attracting tourists and making their experience a pleasurable one. A particular destination may have one, several or many tourist attractions. The more attractions a destination has, the better; they provide variety and give tourists different reasons to visit and to stay for a longer period.
- Accessibility – whether tourists are able to access the location. Accessibility is affected by border and immigration rules, communication and other support infrastructure, and vehicle access.
- Tolerance – the ability of residents to tolerate the presence of visitors who appear to be having a good time.

- Security – currently the most important factor taken into consideration by tourists making travel decisions. Whether security problems (such as crime, civil unrest, terrorism or natural disasters) are real or only perceived, many people will continue to hold entrenched beliefs. Although we know we should not believe everything reported in the media, this is how people get their daily news. Media reports inform people's conversations and influence their thought processes. This will always be the case, so it is very important that destinations avoid bad publicity.

- Living support and comfort systems – all the comfort and support required by tourists when staying at a destination, such as tasty meals and clean accommodation.

- Cost–benefit advantage – the comparison between the costs of experiencing a destination and the benefits of that experience. Some tourists can afford expensive holidays while others are constrained by small budgets. Different tourists weigh up the relative costs and benefits in different ways. For example, one person might consider price to be a very important factor in deciding where to go for a holiday, while another might consider security to be more important than price.

- Information diffusion – distribution of information. No matter what the size of the destination, and regardless of the quality of its products and services, no-one will visit a place if no-one knows about it. Destinations must make adequate information available to potential visitors, through various media channels.

In considering the geography of tourism, we should focus not only on TDRs but also on the other elements, because they are all interrelated. To achieve wider distribution of information and more effective networking, destination organisations should communicate their marketing in all three regions (TGRs, TRs and TDRs). Ideally they should have a presence in all three regions, in order to better direct the flow of tourism traffic.

A tourist destination must be exciting. By providing a variety of activities it will induce tourists to stay longer and spend more money. Kayaking (like surfing, hiking and fishing) can be undertaken in many different countries. What would you do to promote kayaking in PNG as more attractive than kayaking in other countries?

Unit 12.1 Activity 3A: Characteristics of tourist regions – short-answer questions

1. Provide a domestic tourism case and identify TGR, TR and TDR. Describe how tourism has influenced local lives and businesses.
2. Using the diagram 'The tourist area life cycle' on page 102, explain where:
   a. PNG as a tourism destination might fit.
   b. A tourist attraction that you know of might fit.

Education tourism in PNG: a case study

Few Papua New Guineans would immediately think of their universities and other tertiary education institutions as tourist attractions, or of international students as tourists making a contribution to the PNG economy. At the Madang Campus of the Divine Word University (DWU) – one of PNG's fastest-growing universities, with several branches across PNG and the South Pacific – some 15 international students are enrolled in diploma and degree programs. At the time of writing, diploma students from the Solomon Islands are paying K6815 and degree students are paying K8500 in annual tuition fees, while other international students pay full fees of close to K22 800 each year. On average, an international student at DWU in Madang spends about K12 705 in fees and K6000 in living costs per year. In one year, international students contributed a total of K280 575 to the Madang economy alone. The total contribution of international students to the national economy is of course even greater, as would be demonstrated if students at other universities and tertiary institutions in PNG were included in these calculations.

Despite its positive economic effects, education tourism is given little attention in the promotional activities of tourism agencies, with the possible exception of some inbound tour operators who include it among the many attractions that they advertise to potential clients. One reason for this omission might be that international students (and students in general) have not been perceived as tourists, because they don't normally buy or use the types of services and facilities provided to business or holiday visitors. Yet students' spending is spread across economic sectors and benefits a cross-section of local businesses, including individuals in villages, town settlements and residential areas who sell items to supplement their income.

In PNG, the promise of free education is becoming increasingly uncertain, and educational institutions are feeling greater financial pressures. It would be worthwhile for the national tourism agency to explore the potential of attracting more foreign full-fee-paying tertiary students to PNG, to help compensate for local budget cutbacks. This would need to be done in partnership with educational institutions, and would need to consider the need for additional educational infrastructure and the effect on local demand and supply of educational services. As a result, increased international student numbers, attracted by effective promotions by tourist bodies, would contribute to a more robust tertiary sector. Recognition of students as a fully-fledged segment of the tourism sector would lead to a more holistic and effective approach to tourism management.

Unit 12.1 Activity 3B: Education tourism in PNG – short-answer questions

1. Describe why students should be categorised as a segment of the tourism sector.
2. Identify similarities and differences between students and other tourists.
3. What would you consider the advantages and disadvantages of promoting this sector?

Unit 12.2 Tourism as a Business
Topic 1: Business sectors in the tourism industry

There are many different sectors within the tourism industry – businesses that provide goods and services related to tourists. This Unit examines the economic significance and effects of tourism as an industry and looks at the interconnected sectors of hospitality, travel and visitor services. Students are expected to:

- Identify the role of tourism in the economic growth of a country.
- Demonstrate an understanding of the impact of tourism at individual, local, national, regional and global levels.
- Demonstrate an understanding of the principles of good management and customer service.
- Communicate tourism information in a variety of ways and settings.

At the heart of tourism is the tourist, and his or her demand for travel experiences when travelling to a destination. Other sectors come together to cater to this demand.

The diagram on page 107 identifies the operating sectors of the tourism industry. Within this it sets out the public- and private-sector components of the industry that act as **catalyst**, planning, development and promotion organisations that cater to tourists' needs and benefit from this exchange. Brief descriptions are as follows.

- Transportation sector – This comprises airlines, bus companies and so on. It moves people and goods.

- Accommodation sector – This includes all forms of accommodation from modern hotels (Coral Sea chain of hotels, Crown Plaza, Holiday Inn, Airways International Hotel and the Papuan Hotel) to self-contained apartments and long-term stays (for example, Kalibobo Village Resort in Madang); lodges (such as Kimininga Lodge in Mt Hagen); and guest houses and home-stays in rural and urban areas.

- Food services sector – This includes international fast food chains (McDonald's, KFC and Big Rooster in Port Moresby); restaurants as stand-alone facilities or as part of another operation (such as Ang's Restaurant in Gordons, Grand Palace Restaurant and Coffee House in the RH Hypermart in Gordons and Ocean View Restaurant in Madang); independent fast food restaurants; cafeterias and traditional restaurants.

- Attractions sector – This includes many PNG icons: Kokoda Trail, Kalibobo Lighthouse in Madang, Mt Wilhelm in Simbu, Tufi Fjords in Oro, Lae War Cemetery, war wrecks in East New Britain, Black Cat Trail in Morobe, smoked bodies at Aseki in Menyamya, cocoa and copra plantations on the coast, coffee and tea plantations in the Highlands and Mt Bosavi in Eastern Highlands. This sector also includes many natural environments, flora and fauna, and built attractions. Many natural phenomena (the 'fireworks' display from erupting volcanoes; animal migrations) also attract tourists.

- Events sector – This includes cultural festivals held on set dates (the Hiri Moale Festival in Port Moresby, Mt Hagen Cultural Show, New Britain Mask Festival, East Sepik Kundu Festival, Gulf Mini Mask Festival, Simbai Kalam Festival, Goroka Show, Morobe Show in Lae); sporting events (Milne Bay Canoe Festival, surfing competitions, game fishing competitions, South Pacific Games, rugby and football competitions); MICE (meetings, incentives, conferences and exhibitions); religious gatherings; special occasions (Independence, Christmas and New Year celebrations); and other small events in urban and rural areas (bride price and other customary exchanges).

- Adventure and outdoor **recreation** – A number of these activities are developing as tourist needs change: kayaking, canoeing, mountain climbing, trekking, caving, water rafting, boating, bushwalking, cycling and camping. They combine an element of thrill-seeking with being outdoors. A recent interest in this area is ecotourism, which lets tourists get close to nature.

- Entertainment – At the other end of the natural–manufactured spectrum is the equally fast-growing component of entertainment. PNG's capital city, Port Moresby, is also growing as the entertainment capital, in comparison with provincial towns. This sector includes night clubs, hotel bars and lounges that provide entertainment; live performances by bands; traditional live performances to entertain guests; and movie theatres.

- Trade sector and tourism services – The travel trade is made up of retail travel agents and wholesale tour operators. Both are critical to connecting 'experience suppliers' with tourists. Computer support services, retail services, financial services, specialised consulting services and tourism educators all contribute to the smooth running of the complex tourism system. Without these support services, tourism would suffer.

- Spirit of hospitality – Tourists are humans who want to believe that they are truly welcome guests. The operating sectors of tourism are responsible for delivering high-quality, memorable experiences that are customised to provide individual satisfaction.

- Planning, development, promotion and catalyst organisations (PDPCO) – These are the visionaries, policy-makers, strategic planners, and individuals and groups who 'make the right things happen' so that tourism can flourish. In tourism, it is as critical that we 'do the right things' as that we 'do things right'. Policy-makers need to ensure that destinations offer the kinds of travel experiences that are most appropriate to the visitor, while keeping in mind any limitations imposed by the resources of the destination.

In most countries, policy and planning involve two very important categories of stakeholders: the public sector (government) and the **private sector**. At the national level, governments are represented by a national government tourism office (PNG Ministry of Tourism, Arts and Culture – Tourism Promotion Authority or PNGTPA). A national travel-tourism industry **association** typically represents the private sector (PNG Travel Industry Association or PNGTIA).

At the state/provincial level, the public- and private-sector organisations are usually known respectively as the state/provincial government tourism office (in PNG provincial tourism comes under the Department of Commerce, Tourism and Industry) and the state/provincial private travel industry association (e.g. Madang Tourism Association). At the city/municipal or regional/district level there will be authorities dealing with local tourism concerns. More visitor bureaus in PNG are publicly funded than is generally the case overseas.

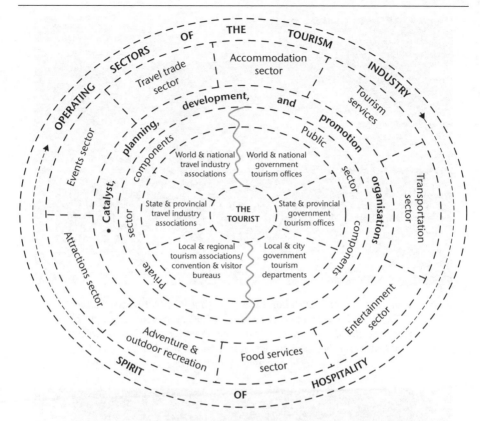

Operating sectors of the tourism industry (adapted with modification from Goeldner & Brent Ritchie 2009)

The 'Asaro mud-man' of Eastern Highlands Province is one of the iconic tourism attractions of PNG. What other PNG tourist attractions would you consider to be symbolic of PNG?

Events such as the multicultural spectacle that is the Mt Hagen Cultural Show attract large numbers of tourists to PNG every year. Research the different cultural shows and festivals held in PNG annually and make a table ranking the numbers of visitors they attract. List the business sectors related to each event.

Travel Air is a new airline in PNG. Locally owned, its motto is 'Mangi Lo Peles'. What benefits can a new airline bring to the tourism industry in PNG?

Unit 12.2 Activity 1: Tourism as a business – short-answer questions

1. Use an example to explain how any two operating sectors of the tourism industry would work together in PNG.

2. Give an example of each of the following types of organisation, and describe its role:

   a. International tourism organisation.

   b. National tourism office.

   c. National travel (tourism) industry association.

   d. Provincial visitors bureau.

   e. Provincial tourism association.

Unit 12.2 Tourism as a Business
Topic 2: The economics of tourism

The previous Topic looked at some of the business sectors in the tourism industry. In Topic 2 we consider the impact of these different sectors on a country's economy, and the wealth and job opportunities that can be created.

Tourism is very important to domestic and world economies. For this reason economists analyse tourism in terms of supply, demand, **balance of payments**, foreign exchange, employment, expenditures, development, **multipliers** and other factors.

Destination countries initiate and maintain tourism development because of the potential for substantial tourism-derived direct revenue. As discussed in Unit 12.1, Topic 1, the WTTC predicted that by the end of 2012 the travel and tourism industry would contribute US$2 trillion (K4.2 trillion) to the global economy, and directly sustain some 100.3 million jobs.

The table below shows summary estimates and forecasts by the WTTC of the total international economic effects of tourism on the world's gross domestic product (GDP), derived from its 2012 annual research.

	2011 (US$ billion)[a]	2011 Proportion of total GDP %	2012 Forecast growth[b] %	2022 (US$ billion)[a]	2022 Forecast proportion of total GDP	2012–2022 Forecast annual growth[c] %
Direct contribution to GDP	1 972.8	2.8	2.8	3 056.2	3.0	4.2
Total contribution to GDP	6 346.1	9.1	2.8	9 939.5	9.8	4.3
Visitor exports	1 170.6	5.3	1.7	1 694.7	4.3	3.6
Domestic spending	2 791.2	4.0	3.5	4 547.6	4.6	4.6
Leisure spending	3 056.9	4.4	3.1	4 853.8	4.8	4.4
Business spending	968.4	1.4	2.5	1 476.2	1.5	4.0
Capital investment	743.0	4.9	3.5	1 320.4	5.1	5.6

	2011 jobs (million)	2011 Proportion of total jobs %	2012 Forecast growth %	2022 jobs (million)	2022 Forecast proportion of total jobs %	2012–2022 Forecast annual growth %
Direct contribution to employment	98.031	3.3	2.3	120.470	3.6	1.9
Total contribution to employment	254.941	8.7	2.0	327.922	9.8	2.3
[a] 2011 constant prices and exchange rates [b] 2012 real growth (NB these figures are adjusted for inflation) [c] 2012–2022 annualised real growth (NB these figures are adjusted for inflation)						

Effects of tourism on world GDP (source: World Travel and Tourism Council 2012)

From these figures we can draw the following conclusions:

- In 2011 the direct contribution of travel and tourism to world GDP was US$1972.8 billion (2.8% of total world GDP). This is forecast to rise by 2.8% in 2012, and by 4.2% each year from 2012, eventually reaching US$3056.2 billion (K6502.55 billion) in 2022 (in constant 2011 prices). The direct contribution of travel and tourism to GDP reflects the internal spending on travel and tourism (total spending on travel and tourism within a particular country, by residents and non-residents for business and leisure purposes) as well as government individual spending (spending by government on travel and tourism services directly linked to visitors – e.g. cultural facilities such as museums and recreational facilities such as national parks).

- In 2011 the total contribution of travel and tourism to GDP was US$6346.1 billion (9.1% of GDP). This is forecast to rise by 2.8% in 2012, and by 4.3% each year from 2012, eventually reaching US$9939.5 billion (K21 147.87 billion) in 2022. The total contribution of travel and tourism includes its wider impacts (the indirect and induced impacts) on the economy. The indirect contribution includes the GDP and jobs supported by:

  - Travel and tourism investment spending – an important aspect of both current and future activity. This includes investments such as the purchase of new aircraft and construction of new hotels.

  - Government collective spending – helps travel and tourism activity in many different ways as it is made on behalf of the community at large, e.g. tourism marketing and promotion, aviation, administration, security services, resort area sanitation services.

  - Domestic purchases of goods and services – by the sectors dealing directly with tourists, e..g. purchases of food and cleaning services by hotels, of fuel and catering services by airlines, and of IT services by travel agents.

  - Induced contribution – measures the GDP and jobs supported by the spending of those who are directly or indirectly employed by the travel and tourism industry.

- In 2011 travel and tourism directly supported 98.031 million jobs (3.3% of total employment). This is expected to rise by 2.3% in 2012 and then by 1.9% per annum to 120.470 million jobs (3.6% of total employment) in 2022. This includes employment by hotels, travel agents, airlines and other passenger transportation services (excluding commuter services). It also includes, for example, those activities of the restaurant and leisure industries that are directly supported by tourists.

- In 2011 the total contribution of travel and tourism to employment, including jobs indirectly supported by the industry, was 254.941 million jobs (8.7% of total employment). This is expected to rise by 2.0% in 2012 to 260.093 million jobs and then by 2.3% per annum to 327.922 million jobs in 2022 (9.8% of total). Total contribution to employment measures the number of jobs generated directly in the travel and tourism industry plus the indirect and induced contributions.

- In 2011 visitor exports generated US$1170.6 billion (5.3% of total exports). This is forecast to grow by 1.7% in 2012, and then by 3.6% per annum reaching USD$1694.7 billion (4.3% of total) in 2022. Visitor exports are the spending within a country by international tourists for both business and leisure trips, including spending on transport.

- Travel and tourism investment in 2011 was US$743.0 billion, or 4.9% of total investment. It should rise by 3.5% in 2012, and then by 5.6% per annum over the next ten years to reach US$1320.4 billion in 2022 (5.1% of total).

- Domestic travel spending generated 70.5% of direct travel and tourism GDP in 2011, compared with 29.5% for visitor exports (foreign visitor spending or international tourism receipts). Domestic travel and tourism spending is the spending within a country by that country's residents for both business and leisure trips. Multi-use consumer durables are not included since they are not purchased solely for tourism purposes.

- Leisure travel spending is expected to grow by 3.1% in 2012 to US$3152.2 billion, and then by 4.4% per annum to reach US$4853.8 billion by 2022. Leisure travel and tourism spending is the spending on leisure travel within a country by residents and international visitors.

- Business travel spending is expected to grow by 2.5% in 2012 to US$993.0 billion, and then by 4.0% per annum to reach US$1476.2 billion in 2022. Business travel and tourism spending is spending on business travel within a country by residents and international visitors.

- Travel and tourism was expected to attract capital investment of US$743.0 billion in 2011. This was expected to rise by 3.5% in 2012, and then by 5.6% per annum over the next ten years to reach US$1320.4 billion in 2022.

- Indirect and induced markets – indirect contribution is the contribution to GDP and jobs of the following three factors:

  - Capital investment – includes capital investment spending by all sectors directly involved in the travel and tourism industry. This also constitutes investment spending by other industries on specific tourism assets such as new visitor accommodation and passenger transport equipment, as well as restaurants and leisure facilities for specific tourism use.

  - Government collective spending – general government spending in support of general tourism activity. This can include national as well as regional and local government spending. For example, it includes tourism promotion, visitor information services, administrative services and other public services.

  - Supply-chain effects – purchases of domestic goods and services directly by different sectors of the travel and tourism industry as inputs to their final tourism output.

- Induced contribution – the broader contribution to GDP and employment of spending by those who are directly or indirectly employed by travel and tourism.

The following tables show, firstly, international tourist arrivals by country of destination, followed by international tourism receipts (in US$ million) by country of destination.

We can see that in 2004 PNG had 59 000 tourist arrivals and receipts of US$18 million (K38.5 million); Fiji had 504 000 tourist arrivals and receipts of US$420 million (K898.4 million); New Caledonia had 100 000 tourist arrivals and receipts of US$241 million (K515.5 million); Cook Islands had 83 000 tourist arrivals and receipts of US$72 million (K154.01 million); and Vanuatu had 50 000 tourist arrivals (2003) and receipts of US$52 million (K111.2 million). Comparing PNG and Vanuatu proportionately, one tourist arrival in PNG in 2004 spent US$305 (K652), whereas one tourist arrival in Vanuatu in 2003 spent US$1040 (K2225).

There is some debate over the accuracy and reliability of tourism figures gathered and reported. Although organisations may adhere to approved methods and protocols in gathering and reporting data, not all countries are up to date and consistent in gathering, recording and presenting data and reports. It is acknowledged that there are difficulties in collecting these data, which further contributes to the problem. Despite this, the information does present interesting facts and implications about the contributions and effects of tourism, the priorities of individual countries and their respective tourism industries.

	Series	International tourist arrivals (1000)						Market share in the region (%)			Change (%)		Average annual growth (%)	
		1990	1995	2000	2003	2004	2005	1990	2000	2005	04/03	05/04	90–00	00–05
Asia and the Pacific		56165	82451	110573	113166	144150	155353	100	100	100	27.4	7.8	7.0	7.0
North-East Asia		26394	41313	58349	61732	79412	87576	47.0	52.8	56.4	28.6	10.3	8.3	8.5
China	TF	10484	20034	31229	32970	41761	46809	18.7	28.2	30.1	26.7	12.1	11.5	8.4
Hong Kong (China)	TF			8814	9676	13655	14773		8.0	9.5	41.1	8.2		10.9
Japan	TF	3236	3345	4757	5212	6138	6728	5.8	4.3	4.3	17.8	9.6	3.9	7.2
Korea, D P Rp	*	115						0.2						
Korea, Republic of	VF	2959	3753	5322	4754	5818	6023	5.3	4.8	3.9	22.4	3.5	6.0	2.5
Macao (China)	TF	2513	4202	5197	6309	8324	9014	4.5	4.7	5.8	31.9	8.3	7.5	11.6
Mongolia	TF	147	108	137	201	301	338	0.3	0.1	0.2	49.4	12.4	-0.7	19.8
Taiwan (pr. of China)	VF		2332	2624	2248	2950	3378		2.4	2.2	31.2	14.5		5.2
South-East Asia		21469	28821	36908	35986	47006	49312	38.2	33.4	31.7	30.6	4.9	5.6	6.0
Brunei Darussalam	VF	377	498	984			815	0.7	0.9	0.5			10.1	-3.7
Cambodia	TF	17	220	466	701	1055	1422	0.0	0.4	0.9	50.5	34.7	39.2	25.0
Indonesia	TF	2178	4324	5064	4467	5321	5002	3.9	4.6	3.2	19.1	-6.0	8.8	-0.2
Lao P.D.R.	TF	14	60	191	196	407	672	0.0	0.2	0.4	107.7	65.1	29.9	28.6
Malaysia	TF	7446	7469	10222	10577	15703	16431	13.3	9.2	10.6	48.5	4.6	3.2	10.0
Myanmar	TF	21	117	208	206	242	232	0.0	0.2	0.1	17.7	-4.0	25.8	2.2
Philippines	TF	1025	1760	1992	1907	2291	2623	1.8	1.8	1.7	20.1	14	6.9	5.7
Singapore	TF	4842	6070	6062	4703	6553	7080	8.6	5.5	4.6	39.3	8.0	2.3	3.2
Thailand	TF	5299	6952	9579	10082	11737	11567	9.4	8.7	7.4	16.4	-1.4	6.1	3.8
Vietnam	VF	250	1351	2140	2429	2928	3468	0.4	1.9	2.2	20.6	18.4	24.0	10.1

	Series	International tourist arrivals (1000)						Market share in the region (%)			Change (%)		Average annual growth (%)	
		1990	1995	2000	2003	2004	2005	1990	2000	2005	04/03	05/04	90–00	00–05
Asia and the Pacific		*56165*	*82451*	*110573*	*113166*	*144150*	*155353*	*100*	*100*	*100*	*27.4*	*7.8*	*7.0*	*7.0*
Oceania		**5152**	**8084**	**9230**	**9023**	**10118**	**10488**	**9.2**	**8.3**	**6.8**	**12.1**	**3.7**	**6.0**	**2.6**
American Samoa	TF	26	34	44			25	0.0	0.0	0.0			5.4	–11.1
Australia	VF/TF	2215	3726	4530	4354	4774	5020	3.9	4.1	3.2	9.6	5.2	7.4	2.1
Cook Islands	TF	34	48	73	78	83	88	0.1	0.1	0.1	6.4	6.1	7.9	3.9
Fiji	TF	279	318	294	431	504	550	0.5	0.3	0.4	17.0	9.1	0.5	13.3
French Polynesia	TF	132	172	252	213	212	208	0.2	0.2	0.1	–0.4	–1.8	6.7	–3.8
Guam	TF	780	1362	1287	910	1160	1228	1.4	1.2	0.8	27.5	5.8	5.1	–0.9
Kiribati	TF	3	4	5	5	4	3	0.0	0.0	0.0	–26.5	–22.4	4.8	–10.3
Marshall Islands	TF	5	6	5	7	9	9	0.0	0.0	0.0	25.2	1.8	0.4	12.0
Micronesia (Fed. St. of)	TF			21	18	19	19		0.0	0.0	6.0	–1.6		–2.0
North Mariana Islands	TF	426	669	517	452	525	498	0.8	0.5	0.3	16.2	–5.1	2.0	–0.7
New Caledonia	TF	87	86	110	102	100	101	0.2	0.1	0.1	–2.4	1.1	2.4	–1.7
New Zealand	VF	976	1409	1787	2104	2334	2366	1.7	1.6	1.5	10.9	1.3	6.2	5.8
Niue	TF	1	2	2	3	3	3	0.0	0.0	0.0	–5.8	9.5	6.6	8.0
Palau	TF	33	53	58	68	95	86	0.1	0.1	0.1	38.9	–9.2	5.8	8.2
Papua New Guinea	TF	41	42	58	56	59	69	0.1	0.1	0.0	4.9	17.3	3.5	3.6
Samoa	TF	48	68	88	92	98	102	0.1	0.1	0.1	6.1	3.7	6.2	3.0
Solomon Islands	TF	9	11	5	7		9	0.0	0.0	0.0			–5.5	12.6
Tonga	TF	21	29	35	40	41	42	0.0	0.0	0.0	2.7	1.6	5.2	3.6
Tuvalu	TF	1	1	1	1	1	1	0.0	0.0	0.0	–6.3	–15.9	1.0	–0.3
Vanuatu	TF	35	44	58	50	61	62	0.1	0.1	0.0	21.9	1.0	5.2	1.4

South Asia		3 150	4 233	6 086	6 426	7 613	7 977	5.6	5.5	5.1	18.5	4.8	6.8	5.6
Bangladesh	TF	115	156	199	245	271	208	0.2	0.2	0.1	10.9	-23.4	5.6	0.9
Bhutan	TF	2	5	8	6	9	14	0.0	0.0	0.0	47.7	47.3	14.3	12.4
India	TF	1 707	2 124	2 649	2 726	3 457	3 919	3.0	2.4	2.5	26.8	13.3	4.5	8.1
Iran	TF	154	489	1 342	1 546	1 659		0.3	1.2		7.3		24.2	
Maldives	TF	195	315	467	564	617	395	0.3	0.4	0.3	9.4	-35.9	9.1	-3.3
Nepal	TF	255	363	464	338	385	375	0.5	0.4	0.2	13.9	-2.6	6.2	-4.1
Pakistan	TF	424	378	557	501	648	798	0.8	0.5	0.5	29.4	23.2	2.8	7.5
Sri Lanka	TF	298	403	400	501	566	549	0.5	0.4	0.4	13.1	-3.0	3.0	6.5

Source: World Tourism Organization (UNWTO) ©

(Data as collected by UNWTO for TMT 2006 edition)

International tourist arrivals by country of destination, 1990–2005 (source: UNWTO November 2006)

	International tourism receipts (US$ million)						Market share in the region (%)			Change (%)		Receipts per arrival[1]	Receipts per capita[1]
	1990	1995	2000	2003	2004	2005	1990	2000	2005	04/03	05/04		US$
Asia and the Pacific	*46 474*	*80 700*	*90 207*	*98 363*	*129 523*	*140 765*	*100*	*100*	*100*	*31.7*	*8.7*	*900*	*36*
North-East Asia	**22 651**	**36 167**	**44 460**	**47 145**	**64 001**	**70 820**	**48.7**	**49.3**	**50.3**	**35.8**	**10.7**	**805**	**42**
China	2 218	8 730	16 231	17 406	25 739	29 296	4.8	18.0	20.8	47.9	13.8	615	20
Hong Kong (China)	4 682	7 760	5 907	7 137	8 999	10 286	10.1	6.5	7.3	26.1	14.3	660	1 313
Japan	3 578	3 224	3 373	8 816	11 269	12 439	7.7	3.7	8.8	27.8	10.4	1 835	88
Korea, D P Rp	29						0.1					375	6
Korea, Republic of	3 559	5 150	6 834	5 358	6 069	5 660	7.7	7.6	4.0	13.3	–6.7	1 045	125
Macao (China)	1 473	3 102	3 208	5 155	7 479	7 757	3.2	3.6	5.5	45.1	3.7	900	16 797
Mongolia	5	21	36	143	185	177	0.0	0.0	0.1	29.4	–4.4	615	67
Taiwan (pr. of China)	1 740	3 286	3 738	2 977	4 054	4 977	3.7	4.1	3.5	36.2	22.8	1 375	178
South-East Asia	**14 479**	**26 981**	**26 210**	**24 587**	**32 184**	**33 403**	**31.2**	**29.1**	**23.7**	**30.9**	**3.8**	**685**	**57**
Cambodia		53	304	389	603	840		0.3	0.6	55.0	39.3	570	45
Indonesia	2 105	5 229	4 975	4 037	4 798	4 521	4.5	5.5	3.2	18.8	–5.8	900	20
Lao P.D.R.	3	51	114	87	119	147	0.0	0.1	0.1	36.7	23.4	290	20
Malaysia	1 667	3 969	5 011	5 898	8 198	8 543	3.6	5.6	6.1	39.0	4.2	520	349
Myanmar	9	151	162	56	84	..	0.0	0.2		50.0		345	2
Philippines	1 306	1 136	2 134	1 545	2 017	2 130	2.8	2.4	1.5	30.6	5.6	880	23
Singapore	4 937	7 646	5 142	3 780	5 219	5 740	10.6	5.7	4.1	38.1	10.0	795	1 199
Thailand	4 326	8 035	7 483	7 856	10 034	10 108	9.3	8.3	7.2	27.7	0.7	855	157
Vietnam	85						0.2						

	International tourism receipts (US$ million)						Market share in the region (%)			Change (%)		Receipts per arrival[1]	Receipts per capita[1]
	1990	1995	2000	2003	2004	2005	1990	2000	2005	04/03	05/04		US$
Oceania	**7315**	**14148**	**14739**	**19902**	**24668**	**26727**	**15.7**	**16.3**	**19.0**	**24.0**	**8.3**	**2435**	**763**
American Samoa	10						0.0						
Australia	4246	8125	9274	12349	15191	16866	9.1	10.3	12.0	23.0	11.0	3180	763
Cook Is	16	28	36	69	72	92	0.0	0.0	0.1	4.3	27.8	865	3396
Fiji	202	291	182	340	420	435	0.4	0.2	0.3	23.3	3.8	840	476
French Polynesia	171			480	553		0.4			15.2		2610	2076
Guam	936						2.0						
Kiribati	1	2	3				0.0	0.0					
Marshall Is		3	4					0.0				665	61
Micronesia (Fed.St.of)			15	17	17	17		0.0	0.0	-1.2	3.6	870	153
N.Mariana Is	455	655					1.0						
New Caledonia	94	108	111	196	241		0.2	0.1	0.1	22.7		2420	1127
New Zealand	1030	2318	2267	3981	4790	4865	2.2	2.5	3.5	20.3	1.6	2050	1199
Niue		2											
Palau			53	76	97	97		0.1	0.1	28.2	0.3	1020	4842
Papua New Guinea	41	25	21	16	18		0.1	0.0	0.0	16.1		310	3
Samoa	20	35	41	54	70	77	0.0	0.0	0.1	29.6	10.0	715	394
Solomon Is	7	16	4	2	4	2	0.0	0.0	0.0	100.0	-50.0		8
Tonga	9	10	7	14	15	11	0.0	0.0	0.0	7.1	-26.7	365	136
Vanuatu	39	45	56	52			0.1	0.1	0.0			1030	261

	International tourism receipts (US$ million)						Market share in the region (%)			Change (%)		Receipts per arrival[1]	Receipts per capita[1]
	1990	1995	2000	2003	2004	2005	1990	2000	2005	04/03	05/04		US$
South Asia	**2029**	**3404**	**4797**	**6729**	**8670**	**9816**	**4.4**	**5.3**	**7.0**	**28.8**	**13.2**	**1140**	**6**
Bangladesh	11	25	50	57	67	70	0.0	0.1	0.0	17.2	4.8	245	0
Bhutan	2	5	10	8	12	19	0.0	0.0	0.0	50.0	48.6	1350	6
India	1513	2581	3460	4463	6121	7356	3.3	3.8	5.2	37.1	20.2	1770	6
Iran	61	67	467	1033	1074		0.1	0.5		4.0		645	16
Maldives	89	211	321	402	471	287	0.2	0.4	0.2	17.2	–39.1	765	1387
Nepal	64	177	158	200	230	132	0.1	0.2	0.1	15.0	–42.7	595	8
Pakistan	156	110	81	122	178	180	0.3	0.1	0.1	45.9	1.1	275	1
Sri Lanka	132	226	248	441	513		0.3	0.3		16.3		905	26

Source: World Tourism Organization (UNWTO) ©

(Data as collected in UNWTO database November 2006)

International tourism receipts in US$ by country of destination, 1990–2005 (source: UNWTO 2006)

The PNG tourism sector review and master plan (2007–2017) – *Growing PNG Tourism as a Sustainable Industry* – predicted that the benefits of implementing the Tourism Development Plan for PNG would bring K1.1 billion in revenue by 2010 and K1.78 billion by 2015. It suggested that those on holiday would spend K363 million in 2010 and K727 million in 2015, and that total employment in tourism would increase by 4800 jobs by 2010 and 13 000 jobs by 2015. Achievement of these goals and implementation of the master plan and the development of PNG's tourism industry all depend on a successful partnership between the government, industry and people of PNG.

It is probable that the 2010 forecasts were achieved because of factors including stable government; strong economic growth in PNG and its export markets; PNGTPA's marketing and promotional activities; an increase in the number and frequency of Air Nuigini's international flights; and the national government's recognition of tourism as an economic sector.

One of tourism's main contributions to the public purse is taxation revenue. Common examples of such taxes, which may or may not apply in PNG's case, include:

- Airport departure taxes.
- Bed (or hotel room) taxes.
- Permits for entry to public attractions such as national parks.
- Entry or transit visas.
- Gaming licenses.

In addition to these taxes, tourists pay for goods and services that are subject to sales tax.

One potentially frustrating aspect of taxation, particularly from the perspective of a destination management or tourism department, is that governments are often happy to 'milk the cash cow', but they make little or no reinvestment in the tourism industry.

Benefits of tourism include:

- Employment opportunities; training; developing particular skills; gaining knowledge of the industry.
- Increased income and much-needed foreign exchange.
- Contribution to GDP (gross domestic product) and GNP (**gross national product**).
- The use of tourist infrastructure (which can be built on existing infrastructure) to stimulate local commerce and meet the local community's recreational needs.
- Creating uses for local products and resources, helping to diversify the local economy.

Costs of tourism, especially related to overdevelopment, can include:

- Added pressure on resources that may already be constrained.
- Inflation caused by demand from tourism.
- Social problems.
- Displacement and restricted access to tourism resources when rules are enforced.
- Commercialising culture, religion and the arts.

One popular concept is the income multiplier effect (IME) of indirect revenue generation. This is a measure of the subsequent income generated in a destination's economy by direct tourist expenditure. The following diagram illustrates this concept:

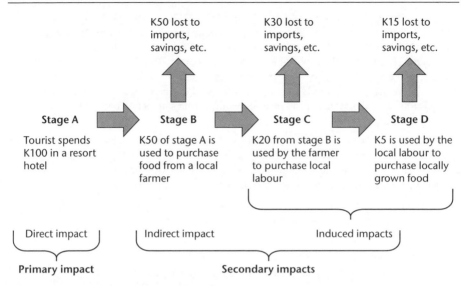

	K50 lost to imports, savings, etc.	K30 lost to imports, savings, etc.	K15 lost to imports, savings, etc.

Stage A ➡ **Stage B** ➡ **Stage C** ➡ **Stage D**

Tourist spends K100 in a resort hotel | K50 of stage A is used to purchase food from a local farmer | K20 from stage B is used by the farmer to purchase local labour | K5 is used by the local labour to purchase locally grown food

Direct impact | Indirect impact | Induced impacts

Primary impact | **Secondary impacts**

The multiplier effect in tourism: a simplified example (source: Weaver & Oppermann 2000)

The initial spending by the tourist is the direct or primary impact. All subsequent circulation of the money spent by the tourist is described as secondary impacts, although within this a distinction is made between the first circulation of that money (the indirect impact) and all the circulations that follow (the induced impacts).

It is important to remember that an economic approach to tourism must not take precedence over other equally important considerations such as environmental consciousness, sociocultural effects, resource integrity and quality, host participation and ethical principles.

When a tourist buys an artefact such as a bilum from a local seller, what is the direct/ primary impact of that spending? What might be its multiplier impact?

The new Grand Papua Hotel in Port Moresby. What would have been its contribution to capital investment in PNG tourism? What might be its continuing contribution to the PNG economy? Should its contribution be regarded in terms of the tourism industry only? Give reasons for your answers.

Unit 12.2 Activity 2: Tourism as a business

1. Give definitions for the following terms:
   a. Gross domestic product (GDP).
   b. Gross national product (GNP).
   c. Balance of payments.
   d. Foreign reserves.
   e. Direct contribution by travel and tourism to GDP.
   f. Direct contribution by travel and tourism to employment.
   g. Total contribution by travel and tourism to GDP.
   h. Visitor exports.
   i. Government individual spending.
   j. Induced contribution.
2. Use a simple example to explain the principles described in the diagram 'The multiplier effect in tourism', on page 122.

Unit 12.2 Tourism as a Business

Topic 3: Business operations and employment opportunities

The previous Topic looked at some of the business sectors in the tourism industry. In Topic 3 we consider the effects of these different sectors on a country's economy, and the wealth and job opportunities that can be created.

Business operations in tourism

In deciding to go into the tourism business, one needs to ask key questions. Success in the tourism business is largely dependent on being suited to self-employment. The following personal qualities are important:

- Motivation – interest in and commitment to succeeding.
- Ability – one's capacities and talents.
- Knowledge of where to concentrate one's efforts.
- Vision – a clear road map to success.

Considerations for tourism businesses include:

- The tourism business is a people business. Do you like and want to serve people?
- There is a lead-time of up to five years for establishing a successful tourism business.
- There may be an initial period of slow trading, when potential customers are still unaware of your business's existence and the services you offer.
- It can take up to three years for a venture to become profitable, and for you to build up a solid professional reputation. Meanwhile investment costs can be mounting.
- It is dangerous to over-specialise (by focusing on one product, service or market segment). A business may be at risk if its specialisation is threatened or no longer viable.
- Businesses are vulnerable to external shocks. They must be able to face and handle changes in the **external – or macro – environment**).
- Personal preparedness is essential. You need a well-researched business plan and proposal for a loan, and perhaps an equity partner.
- Your skills, commitment, financial contribution and understanding of business needs are all important.

There are two ways of entering the tourism business as an entrepreneur: you can start a new enterprise or buy an existing one. Starting up your own business means that you are in control of investment and growth in your business; buying an existing business may involve higher purchase costs but might offer instant income.

One must also be aware of **legal** requirements. In PNG all companies are registered through the IPA (Investment Promotion Authority) in Port Moresby. There are specific forms and requirements for company registration. Information can also be obtained from the provincial commerce, tourism and industry office and on the IPA website: www.ipa.gov.pg. Some information is provided here:

Company incorporation (citizen and non-citizen)	
Application for registration	K450
Application to reserve name	K50
Total	K500
Business name incorporation	
Application fee	K50
Renewal	K40
Form 4, 5, 7, 8 or 9	K5
Form 6	K10
Availability name search	K10
Certified certificate copy	K8
Search fee	K10
Extract fee	K10

Fees payable to the Registrar of Companies (source: Papua New Guinea Investment Promotion Authority www.ipa.gov.pg)

Form 1. Application to register a company
Form 2. Consent of director of proposed company
Form 3. Consent of secretary of proposed company
Form 4. Consent of shareholder of proposed company
Form 6. Application for reservation of a company name
Form 7. Application to change name of a company
Form 9. Notice of adoption, alteration or revocation of constitution
Form 10. Notice of issue of shares
Form 11. Notice of redemption or acquisition of shares by company
Form 13. Notice of change of shareholder (share transfer)
Form 14. Notice of location or change of share register of listed company divided into two or more registers (share transfer)
Form 15. Consent and certificate of director (existing company)
Form 16. Notice of change of directors and particulars of directors

Form 17. Notice of change of registered office
Form 18. Notice of location of records not kept at registered office
Form 19. Notice of change of address for service
Form 20. Consent of secretary (existing company)
Form 21. Notice of appointment or change of secretaries or particulars of secretaries
Form 22. Annual return
Form 23. Notice of shareholding in company
Form 24. Notice for registration of charge
Form 25. Certificate of compliance with *Stamp Duties Act*
Form 26. Notice of issue of further debentures in a series
Form 27. Notice of property acquired by company or overseas company while property subject to a charge
Form 28. Notice in respect to charge created before registration as an overseas company
Form 29. Notice of assignment or variation of charge
Form 31. Notice of partial or total satisfaction of registered charge

Form 32. Notice of release or disposal of charged property Form 33. Application for registration of amalgamation proposal Form 36. Notice of appointment of receiver Form 37. Notice of registration or disqualification of receiver Form 38. Notice of end of receivership Form 39. Notice of appointment of liquidator Form 41. Notice of resignation or disqualification of liquidator Form 43. Form of claim by unsecured creditor Form 45. Request to remove company from register	Form 46. Application for registration of overseas company Form 48. Notice of change of name of overseas company Form 49. Notice of change in constitution of overseas company Form 50. Notice of change in directors or resident agents of overseas company Form 51. Notice of change in address of principal places of business in Papua New Guinea of overseas company Form 52. Annual return of overseas company Form 53. Notice of cessation of business or deregistration or appointment of liquidator to overseas company
Business names forms Form 1. Application for registration of business name Form 3. Statement for renewal of registration of business name Form 4. Statement of change in certain particulars Form 5. Notice of cessation of business under business name Form 6. Statement of change of persons in relation to whom business name is registered	**Foreign enterprises – certification forms** Form 3. Application for certification by a foreign enterprise Form 5. Application by a foreign enterprise for variation of the terms or conditions of a Certificate issued under Section 29 **Patents** Form 1. Request for grant of patent or utility model certificate
Business group forms Forms A–D. Business group application for incorporation Form 6. Business group statement of assets and liabilities **Association forms** Form 1. Notice of intention to apply for the incorporation of an association Form 2. Application for the incorporation of an association Form 4. Application for approval to a change of name Form 6. Notice of appointment of a public officer Form 7. Notice of passing of special resolution to which Section 9 applies Form 8. Notice of passing of special resolution for amalgamation of associations	**Intellectual Property Office of Papua New Guinea** **Trademarks** Form 2. Application for amendment or alteration of the register under Section 11 of the Act Form 3. Application to alter a registered trade mark Form 4. Application for registration of trade mark Form 5. Notice of opposition under Section 12 or 40 of the Act Form 6. Application for renewal of registration of trademark Form 7. Application for registration of registered user Form 8. Application for renewal of registration of registered user Form 9. Application for variation or extension of registration of registered user

Industrial designs	Form 10. Application for cancellation of
Form 5. Application for registration of industrial design	registration of registered user
Form 7. Recording of change in ownership	Form 11. Application by person entitled by assignment or transmission to register trademark for registration

Forms required under the Companies Act 1997 *(source: Papua New Guinea Investment Promotion Authority www.ipa.gov.pg)*

An entrepreneur (proprietor or businessperson) should ensure that their business complies with legal requirements in the following areas:

- Environmental protection.
- Workers compensation.
- Trading hours.
- Insurance.
- Workers health and safety.

Other aspects of law relevant to the tourism industry include:

- Contracts – agreements between two or more parties that bind them to certain rights, duties and obligations; *binding* meaning enforceable under law; contracts can be written, oral or valid as observed by the actions of the parties.
- Agency law – implies that the company is responsible for its employees when they are acting on behalf of the company; owners should be familiar with several types of agency authority such as employees' and subcontractors' agency relationships with the company.
- Product liability – general liability or obligation of a producer or supplier of a good or service to make restitution for loss associated with its use, such as personal injury or property damage.
  - Historically in the US and during medieval times in Europe, the law was based on *caveat emptor* or 'let the buyer beware'; in other words the buyer had to rely on his or her own judgement and could not hold a seller liable.
  - The burden has since shifted to *caveat venditor* or 'let the seller beware', due largely to pressure from consumer groups and advocates.
  - Today, any company producing a product of any kind needs product liability insurance to protect itself against potential litigation, even when the company provides warranties.
- Implied warranties – present where no warranty protects a buyer who is injured.
  - For example, an implied warrant of merchantability is that the product does what the producer claims it will do (free from defects; of satisfactory and acceptable quality).
  - Companies need to provide clear instructions on use and warnings about the consequences of misuse.
- **Truth in advertising and marketing strategy** – protects consumers against false or misleading advertising.
  - Advertising must accurately represent what a product can do; must not offer a 'reduced' or 'sale' price on an item that was never advertised at a higher price; must not use list price as a comparison if the business has never sold the item at the list price; must not use bait-and-switch techniques to lure customers into the store only to switch them to buying a higher-priced item.

- Privity of contract – Travel agents and tour operators, while acting as mere agents, have no responsibility for the contract between the travel supplier and the client. But they can be held liable if they provide false information or mislead the client.
- Price discrimination and pricing strategy – Businesses should not sell the same product to different customers at different prices, without justification.
- **Negligence** – breach of duty of care that results in loss or injury to the person or **entity** to whom the duty is owed.

One problem experienced in the tourism business is **rescission** – returning a product for a refund. A supplier often cannot refund a travel product because the defect is observed as the product is consumed; you cannot return time occupying a hotel room, plane or cruise ship; nor can a customer return food or beverage after it has been consumed. One way to avoid such complications relating to liability for **damages** in contract and **tort** can be avoided by carefully wording the terms of standard contract documentation. (Tort generally refers to private – as opposed to public – and civil – as opposed to criminal – offences for which law may provide monetary compensation to the aggrieved party as a **remedy**.)

In international business, most countries around the world recognise four broad legal classifications of companies:

- Sole proprietorship – a single owner running a business.
- Partnership – an association of two or more persons who co-own a business, sharing in the profits and general liability.
- **Corporation** – a separate legal entity that is created to conduct business; has shareholders who own a part of the company and earn dividends.
- Limited liability company – combines **limited liability** of a corporation with the pass-through tax advantages of a partnership, plus the flexibility of a less formal structure.

Factors to be considered in choosing the appropriate form include the level of liability protection required, the operating requirements and the applicable tax strategy. The process for company incorporation in PNG has been simplified so that these four legal classifications no longer apply. An applicant simply fills in the required application forms and submits them, along with the relevant fees, to IPA in Port Moresby. If the application meets all the requirements IPA issues a certificate of company incorporation.

There are different ways in which tourism businesses work together as an industry. Some are described here:

- Principal–agent links – Principals (e.g. airlines and hotels) own the tourism resource, whereas agents sell on their behalf. The link is important because the agent helps to sell the principal's product in the agent's locale. This is convenient for the principal and enables agents to earn commissions on sales.
- Packaged tour arrangements – Packaged tours are typically created by travel agents or tour organisers and require cooperation by at least three parties, typically carrier and accommodation units brought together by a managing unit.
- Reservation systems – There may be common reservation systems used by the tourism industry, e.g. integrated airline and hotel booking systems.
- Cooperative research and development – This is another characteristic of the tourism industry. Companies work together on projects such as the joint USA–Europe development of 'Apollo', a computer reservation system (CRS). Associations such as PATA (Pacific Asia

Travel Association) undertake cooperative marketing research. PATA also markets and promotes the products and services of its members and provides them with reports on market trends.

- Standardised products – Coordinated product design among superficially competitive organisations is becoming more common in the travel and tourism industries, e.g. similar rooms in the same accommodation category; aircrafts flying similar routes to the same locations use similar aircraft and in-flight facilities; meals on board may be produced in the same kitchen. Standardised products lead to a higher order of cooperation and industrialisation.

- Graded products – Graded products, such as the ranking system for accommodation (standard, deluxe, four-star, five-star and so on) function as service assurances to a traveller or agent who has not seen or used the facility before.

- Cooperative pricing policies – Tourist suppliers tend to cooperate in subtle ways on pricing policies, in order to prevent price fluctuations that might make customers feel uncertain about value. For example in PNG most tour guides receive similar pay; bus hires for tourists cost the same amount of money; rural guest houses charge more or less the same amount per night; and airlines try to match a new fare introduced by another airline.

Tourism is an industry made up of many different sectors working together to meet the needs and expectations of a common client: the tourist. It is in the best interest of industry members to understand and recognise these relationships and to cooperate in ways that will enhance the industry's performance and enable it to prosper.

If you decide to set up a guest house, what factors should you consider? Think about the following considerations and prepare a comprehensive summary of what you need to take into account: registration, signage, contact address, environment, amenities and facilities, revenue potential.

Unit 12.2 Activity 3A: Business operations in tourism

Provide the appropriate term for each of the following situations:

A taxi driver drives recklessly, causing his passenger, a tourist, to have chest pains.	
A cleaner leaves a lodge floor wet after mopping but does not put up a sign. A tourist walks on the floor and slips, injuring his ankle.	
Your mum owns and manages her own business.	
This legal entity is separate from its owners, can sue and be sued, acquire and sell real property, maintain perpetual succession, have a corporate seal, lend money, and make and alter its own bylaws.	
A tourist complains to her lawyer that her hotel had low water pressure. She wants to sue her travel agent. The lawyer advises her that she is trying to sue the wrong person.	
A carver is selling a carving for K25 to a local tourist. He sees a foreign tourist coming and quickly raises the price to K50.	

Unit 12.2 Activity 3B: Business operations in tourism – short-answer questions

1. Give an example of cooperation in the tourism industry.
2. If you were to start a tourism business at the village level, what are some considerations?
3. What are the advantages and disadvantages of starting your own business, compared to buying an existing business?

Employment opportunities in tourism

It has been claimed that tourism is the world's largest industry, in terms of the size of its workforce. It employs tens of millions of people, while many others aspire to gain employment in what is often seen as a glamorous industry. In PNG there is a demand for tourism courses in both private and public schools. Recent developments in PNG's **resource sector**, supported by the national government, have further encouraged our educational institutions to offer courses and training to students who wish to join the tourism workforce.

Following are some general characteristics of tourism employment in PNG. These are similar across the world.

- Tourism requires both management and operational staff. Managerial jobs tend to be associated with sales and marketing, while the majority of positions are front-line staff (customer contact employees).
- Salaries are low compared to many other industries. However, pay does increase as one moves up the ladder of seniority.
- Management salaries and benefits are reasonable, although they depend on the size and location of the organisation.

- Many jobs let staff earn extra money through commissions, bonuses and other performance-related incentives.
- The majority of jobs in PNG are in Port Moresby, where the cost of living is high and can be challenging for employees on lower pay.
- Some organisations, such as hotels, allow employees to live on the premises, meaning they do not have to pay for living accommodation.
- The industry has high **staff turnover**, particularly in the hospitality sector.
- Most job advertisements ask for experience rather than formal qualifications.
- Job advertisements tend to emphasise the generic skills and personal qualities of applicants, particularly enthusiasm, **dynamism**, and the ability to work under pressure.

Job title	Brief job description
Bartender or waiter	Bartenders and waiters serve food and beverages to guests of restaurants, hotels, casinos and other hospitality establishments. Additionally, these professionals engage guests for the purpose of ensuring a positive customer experience.
Hotel desk attendant	A desk attendant welcomes all hotel guests and checks them into their rooms. These individuals also provide general information regarding the facility and the area as requested.
Taxi driver	Taxi drivers provide transportation to those who are unable to drive themselves. Charging either a meter or flat rate, these professionals maintain a detailed knowledge of points of interest in the area.
Travel agent	The travel agent helps customers understand their travel, lodging and activity options, in addition to making reservations or purchasing tickets for everything from airline flights to car rentals. Agents must have an understanding of one or more of the reservations technologies used in the industry: Sabre, Amadeus, Worldspan or Galileo. They must also be good at selling and customer relations. More and more agents are getting a formal education in their field and getting certified by the Institute of Certified Travel Agents.
Tour guide	Tour guides escort visitors through landmarks and other points of interest. In addition to providing direction, these professionals also educate visitors on topics such as history and interesting facts regarding the landmark.
Restaurant manager	Manages the daily operations of a restaurant. May require an associate's degree in a related area or its equivalent and at least four years of experience in the field or in a related area. Familiar with a variety of the field's concepts, practices and procedures. Relies on experience and judgement to plan and accomplish goals. Performs a variety of complicated tasks. May lead and direct the work of others. Typically reports to a senior manager. A wide degree of creativity and latitude is expected.

Executive chef	An alternative title for this position might be 'boss of the kitchen'. People in this position oversee everything from purchasing and menu planning to the details of food preparation. Before you reach this level, you will have to grind through years in lower-level food-preparation jobs. If you aspire to this level, you would be well advised to attend a culinary institute.
Concierge	This is the person at the hotel who focuses solely and relentlessly on making his or her employer's guests happy. You'll be arranging for guests' dry cleaning, theatre ticket purchases, restaurant reservations, and more. To do this job, you've got to love serving guests, be a creative problem-solver, and know everything there is to know about your location.
Lodging manager	People in these positions manage the day-to-day operations of a hotel or motel. This means doing everything from managing the housekeeping, room service and reservations staff to managing the supplies purchasing and inventory control. In addition, the lodging manager is ultimately accountable for anything that goes wrong at the hotel or motel, meaning that people in this position can be on call 24/7 for emergencies that range from computer breakdowns to on-site accidents.
Meeting/event planner	People in these positions plan meetings or special events (e.g. company parties or industry conventions) for businesses and other organisations. They do everything from reserving hotel space for meeting or event participants to arranging catering to negotiating rates and contracts with those hotels and caterers and other vendors.
Corporate travel manager	People in this job typically work for big companies, in what is basically an in-house travel-agent position. In addition to handling reservations and ticket-purchasing responsibilities, some corporate travel managers are responsible for creating and maintaining corporate travel policies (which codify things like the rates that various levels of employees can pay for airline tickets and hotels, or which car rental companies employees can use).
Catering manager	A catering manager is the person who manages the day-to-day operations of catering services in a restaurant, hotel, resort or any other part of the hospitality industry. Leading a team of chefs and catering assistants, a catering manager is responsible for optimising the quality of the food, service and performance of their outlets. The most important part of the job is achieving good quality at low cost and maintaining high standards of hygiene and customer satisfaction.

(continued)

Job title	Brief job description
Fitness/leisure centre manager	The leisure industry is dynamic and fast moving and the nature of career opportunities in the industry is changing and growing rapidly. Fitness and leisure centre managers ensure that customers have the best possible experience and are responsible for the efficient day-to-day control of all the centre's activities, ranging from human resources to marketing. They tend to every aspect of the day-to-day running of fitness and leisure centres, both as a service and as a business. Duties include managing staff recruitment and training, dealing with fitness provision and ensuring that health and safety standards are met.
Holiday representative	Holiday representatives work in hotels and holiday resorts across the world. Their role revolves around providing customer service for holiday-makers. They are the main point of contact for clients. Positions are not always permanent; most holiday representatives work a season or have part-time or short-term contracts.
Hotel manager	A hotel manager manages the day-to-day operations of a hotel, including reservations, food services, housekeeping and conventions. In a small hotel, one manager usually makes all the important daily decisions, whereas in a large establishment, a general manager hires a number of managers to be in charge of individual departments.
Tourism officer	A tourism officer works to develop and enhance the visitor facilities of a region and to stimulate tourism growth in order to produce economic benefits for a particular region or site. They often work for local authorities but may also work in private companies or other public sector agencies.

The nature and characteristics of tourism jobs (sources include www.ehow.com, http://gradireland.com & www.wetfeet.com)

The table above describes the nature and characteristics of some tourism jobs.

There are some human resource challenges in the tourism industry today. The major concerns are as follows:

- High staff turnover – Many tourism organisations find it difficult to attract and retain high-performing staff, due to low pay, discriminatory practices, long hours, lack of clear career paths and poor working conditions.
- Managing diversity – It is necessary to manage people of diverse nationality, culture, age and gender.
- Jobs or careers? – Many people tend to view jobs in tourism as short-term, seasonal, part-time or casual, with few long-term prospects. There is little training provided on the job and the relatively flat structures of many organisations means there is less chance of promotion.

- Unethical practices – These may include staff expecting **tips** or **gratuities** from customers to make up for an inadequate salary, or industry exploitation of less fortunate employees.
- Lack of training and education – This has been a problem in PNG for some time, but more recently, technical and vocational institutions and colleges as well as secondary schools have introduced tourism studies into their curriculums.

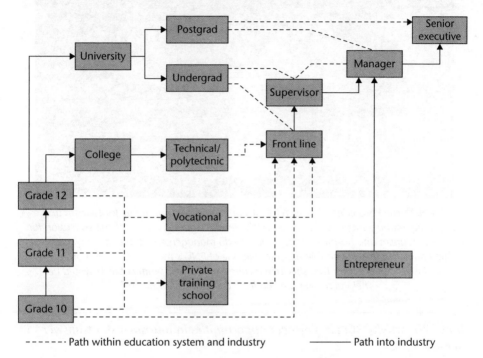

------ Path within education system and industry   ——— Path into industry

Career paths in the PNG tourism industry

The diagram above shows career paths in the tourism industry in PNG. While this model will not apply to everyone, it does present clear career paths for those who are interested.

As a service industry, tourism is dependent on the quality of its human resources. Tourism is seen as a glamorous industry and many people aspire to enter it. But once employed, many leave, giving the industry its reputation for high staff turnover, although this is not true of all sectors or establishments.

One factor in PNG at the moment is the booming economy caused by higher international commodity prices. Investment in the resources sector has led to many new projects, which need to attract staff. This can lead people to leave their tourism jobs in search of greener pastures with better pay and conditions.

Employment in PNG's tourism industry will remain a challenge for the foreseeable future.

Through the PNG education system, Grade 12 students can apply for tourism and hospitality management studies at university level, or gain entry to college education for studies in tourism and hospitality then apply to do management studies at university level. Such qualifications will enable them to join one of PNG's most exciting and promising industries. In addition to a specialised course in tourism, what subjects would be helpful to prepare you for a career in this industry?

Unit 12.2 Activity 3C: Employment opportunities in tourism – short-answer questions

1. Give reasons for the high staff turnover (people leaving jobs) in the tourism industry, particularly in the hospitality sector.

2. What are some unethical practices in the tourism industry?

3. Explain why you would or would not like to work in the tourism industry.

Unit 12.3 Customer Service
Topic 1: Introduction

This Unit focuses on the knowledge and skills required to identify customer product and service requirements. It includes the needs and expectations of customers and the delivery of quality customer service. Topic 1 looks at the definition of customer service. Students are expected to:

- Demonstrate an understanding of tourism at the local, national, regional and international levels.
- Demonstrate an understanding of the principles of good management and customer service.
- Communicate tourism information in a variety of ways and settings.

Defining customer service

In business it is said that 'the customer is king'. Without customers there is no business and it is imperative that businesses organise themselves to serve customers better. It is customers' expenditure that keeps businesses running and people employed. In today's world where there is so much competition and customers are so sophisticated (highly experienced, discerning and demanding), companies use superior customer service as one aspect of **differentiation** (to set their business, products and services apart from those of their rivals in order to be noticed). In the simplest terms, customer service is everything that is done to enhance customer satisfaction.

So, what is a customer? A customer can be defined as 'a person, work-team, business or other type of organisation which buys or utilises goods and services from another' (ACTRAC/ANTA 1996). A customer is not just the person who buys goods and services from an organisation; there are internal customers as well as external customers. Internal customers can be 'a person, group or team in an organisation to whom completed work is passed by fellow workers' (ACTRAC/ANTA 1996). For example, a purchasing manager in a hotel, who buys stock for the hotel and delivers it to various departments based on their requisitions, is providing a service to internal customers such as the restaurant manager and the lodging manager. External customers can be defined as 'the buyers of goods and services who are not employed by, or associated with, the selling organisation' (ACTRAC/ANTA 1996). These include shoppers, tourists, hotel guests, event planners, corporate clients and the like.

It is important to understand that offering customer service does not end at the first instance of providing a good or service to a customer. It covers the full range of help and support offered to a customer before and after a sale has been made. Because service is intangible, meaning that a service cannot be physically examined, checked or tested before it is consumed, the customer experience, if it is to result in customer satisfaction, must be properly managed to create lasting, memorable experiences.

As illustrated in the diagram below, consumption of tourism products and services takes place in three phases:

- Pre-consumption – includes the reservation process.
- Consumption – the time during which the actual service is experienced, for example, when a tourist is on a vacation or a restaurant customer is eating a meal.
- Post-consumption – includes the manner in which the organisation deals with any customer complaints and follows up to find out whether the customer is satisfied.

Customer satisfaction is the difference between customer expectations and service performance. It is whether the customer got what he or she expected that results in either customer satisfaction or dissatisfaction. If the service performance exceeded the customer's expectations, the customer is likely to remain a **loyal customer** who will speak positively to others about the organisation.

Consumption of tourism products and services: a simple three-phase model

Thus, customer satisfaction is important to organisations, as illustrated in the diagram below. Satisfied customers become repeat (regular) customers. They also give positive recommendations to their friends and other people to buy from the organisation. All this increases profits to the organisation, as a result of both greater revenue and lower advertising costs.

But how do we manage the service consumption process? Here are a few strategies to put into action some of the seemingly intangible aspects of service:

* Pre-consumption phase – Create strong brands; provide accessible information; set up a toll-free number for inquiries and bookings; use a central reservation system; use referral/booking agents.
* Consumption time – Employ neat and well-groomed staff dressed in uniforms; staff should be knowledgeable and should always provide a proper greeting; have clean furniture and appropriate lighting; use fresh ingredients; provide fast service.
* Post-consumption phase – Seek customer feedback on the service you have provided; thank customers; deal with any complaints in a prompt, professional and courteous manner; follow up with emails or newsletters containing product offers (if the customer agrees to receive these).

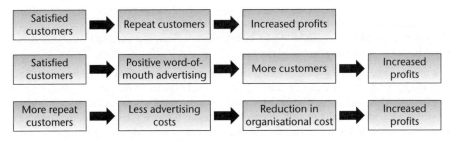

The importance of customer satisfaction

The onus is on the organisation to maintain long-term relationships with its customers. For this reason, many organisations have moved beyond simply providing customer service to establishing and maintaining customer relationships. Relationship marketing is about creating, maintaining and enhancing strong relationships with the customer, with the aim of delivering long-term value to the customer and thus ensuring long-term customer satisfaction.

Providing quality service and welcoming our guests create a good image and leave our guests with fond memories and a feeling of satisfaction.

Unit 12.3 Activity 1: Customer service – short-answer questions

1. What are some tangible aspects of service?

2. What are some intangible aspects of service?

3. Give examples of activities that occur in the pre-consumption phase, consumption time, and post-consumption phase.

4. What activities can an organisation undertake to maintain long-term, satisfied customers?

Unit 12.3 Customer Service
Topic 2: Needs of various tourist groups

In the previous Topic we looked at definitions of customer service. We now consider the different types of customer as represented by the differences between various tourist groups, and their particular needs.

Identifying types of customer

Good customer service results from the product or service offered by the organisation meeting or exceeding the customer's expectations. It is therefore the customer, not the organisation, who determines the level of customer service. To be successful, organisations must strive to provide a level of service that satisfies or exceeds the unique needs of each customer. The organisation needs to know and understand its customers and their expectations before it can offer them the most appropriate level of service.

From various studies and surveys undertaken by the Papua New Guinea Tourism Promotion Authority (1999), the following characteristics of Japanese tourists emerge:

- They are more group oriented than Americans and Europeans, but travel more as individuals than do the residents of most other Asian countries.
- Their obsession with punctuality dictates that even leisure activities must follow a set schedule.
- They like to travel on pre-arranged tours and to receive detailed schedules beforehand.
- They like to spend money, especially on artefacts and other products, all of which must be of good quality.
- They are very cautious and selective about the type of food eaten in hotels.
- They are interested in soft-adventure tourism, historical sites, art galleries and museums, botanical gardens, flora and fauna, sun and surfing.
- Travelling abroad is an intrinsic part of expressing and maintaining one's position in Japanese society.
- More of the younger generation (20–30 years of age) are travelling. These people have higher disposal incomes and the government now allows more annual leave.
- The Japanese are very active while travelling. They take shorter holidays during which they try to cover as many destinations as possible.

David Bojanic, in his study of the modernised family life cycle (FLC) and overseas travel by US citizens, analysed each stage in the FLC (Bojanic 1992):

- Bachelor – younger, single people not concerned about children; want to be with other young adults; like beaches, nightlife and exciting, adventurous activities.
- Newly married – couples with no plans yet for children; mostly interested in accommodations and restaurants, but still like beach resorts that offer many activities and are slightly adventurous.
- Full nest 1 – families who plan their holidays around their children; still prefer beaches and are interested in accommodation and restaurants; shopping facilities considered important.
- Full nest 2 – the children are older and unlikely to accompany their parents on vacations; beaches, accommodations and restaurants still important.

- Empty nest – marks the beginning of later adulthood; more discretionary income and time to travel; look for quality accommodations/restaurants; prefer established resorts.
- Solitary survivors – widowed people; travel to friendly countries; prefer **group tours**, tour guides and bargain shopping.
- Single parent – children not important in vacation planning; prefer beaches and good accommodation and restaurants.
- Middle-aged couples without children – enjoy historical sites and experiencing local customs; want good accommodation and restaurants; travel overseas a great deal and have enough discretionary income to afford expensive accommodation.

Not all destinations are alike; nor are all people alike. Therefore it is necessary to segment the market and determine the salient attributes and product/destination characteristics of each segment. It is also useful to understand the varying levels of loyalty between traveller segments, which is manifested as return trips. The largest segment of visitors to PNG is business travellers. The value of corporate clients and business travellers to any hotel is significant. Following are some of the benefits they can bring to hotels they may patronise:

- Rate – expenses paid for by their employer or sponsoring organisation.
- F&B (food and beverage) – heavy use of fine dining, high-quality wines, liquor and cigarettes.
- Telephone – high use of telephones, including sending faxes.
- Laundry – frequent usage of laundry services in order to maintain their professional appearance.
- Housekeeping – their predictable schedules and patterns of use decrease work for housekeepers.
- Minibars – the heaviest users of minibars.
- Bell service – ask relatively few questions, placing less demand on the concierge or bell captain.

The challenge is to convince business travellers that they need the resort as much as the resort needs them! Cateora (1983) proposed some selling styles based on supposed national characteristics:

- In Asian countries, where people dislike arrogance and displays of extreme self-confidence, vendors should make modest, rational, down-to-earth claims. A vendor should avoid winning an argument against a buyer, who could react negatively to this loss of face.
- In Italy, a lack of self-confidence is perceived as indicating a lack of personal credibility and reliability. For this reason one needs to argue strongly in order to be taken seriously.
- In Great Britain, a soft-sell approach is advisable; a vendor should not be pushy with a prospective buyer.
- In Germany, a hard sell is more effective. Vendors should make visits, offer trials and maintain a strong presence.
- When selling to a Mexican buyer, one should emphasise price.
- In Venezuela, emphasise the quality of the goods for sale.

There are regional variations within PNG. In the Highlands, for example, people like to bargain for items and push for a sale, while in coastal areas such as Madang, sellers stick to their price and are not keen on bargaining.

Every style of selling exists in every culture, but the one used by the majority of sellers will become a modal characteristic by virtue of its frequency. This raises another question: how are customer expectations formed? Generally, these are based on past buying experiences, friends' and associates' opinions, and marketer and competitor information and promises.

In order to retain customers, organisations develop relationship programs with customers:

- Basic – The organisation sells the product or service but does not follow up in any way.
- Reactive – The organisation sells the product or service and encourages the customer to call whenever he or she has any problems or questions.
- Accountable – The organisation communicates with the customer after the sale in order to raise its level of service.
- Proactive – The salesperson calls the customer from time to time, seeking suggestions for improvement.
- Partnership – The organisation works continuously with customers to discover ways of delivering better value.

Destinations and organisations in the tourism industry can use these approaches to deliver long-term value and maintain their clients. When tourists feel that the organisation shows a genuine concern for their interests, they will return and tell others to do the same. This will help promote a positive image of the destination, which attracts more visitors.

Backpackers are adventurous tourists who usually explore rural locations, although being constrained by budget they seek out cost-effective means of travel and accommodation. Hence they are likely to use affordable local facilities such as rural guest houses.

Unit 12.3 Activity 2: The needs of various tourist groups – short-answer questions

1. Suggest some needs of the following types of tourists:
   a. Backpacker.
   b. Birdwatcher.
   c. Mountain climber.
   d. Researcher.
2. Identify three other types of tourists and their needs.
3. What steps could your organisation undertake in order to serve the following clients:
   a. German.
   b. Japanese.
   c. British.

Unit 12.3 Customer Service
Topic 3: Social and interpersonal skills in the workplace

In this Unit so far, we have considered definitions of customer service and the importance of catering for the needs of different tourist groups. In Topic 3 we examine the kinds of social and interpersonal skills that are required in the tourism workplace. The Topic concludes with a case study.

Describing workplace social and interpersonal skills

The world today is described as a 'global village'; many physical barriers have been reduced or removed, allowing the flow of goods, commodities, information, services and people across frontiers. This has led to the **hybridisation** of cultural forms and workplace diversity.

An essential aspect of workplace social and **interpersonal skills** is communication. The diagram below shows a simple communication model consisting of the sender-receiver; the message; the channel; barriers or interference to communication (noise); the receiver-sender; and the feedback. These and other elements of communication are included in the brief descriptions that follow.

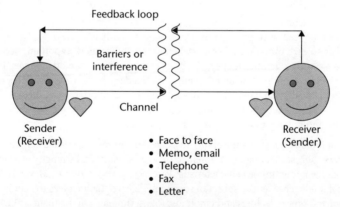

A simple communication model

- Sender–receiver – Interpersonal communication involves at least two persons. Each person formulates and sends messages (source functions) and also perceives and comprehends messages (receiver functions). Personal characteristics and experiences will influence this process.
- Encoding–decoding – Encoding is the act of producing a message (e.g. speaking or writing) and decoding is the act of understanding a message (e.g. listening or reading). Both participants do this.
- Competence – This is the ability to communicate effectively, e.g. knowing what to say to whom in a given context. Interpersonal competence includes knowing how to adjust your communication according to the context of the interaction, the audience with whom you are interacting, and other factors.

- Messages – Signals that serve as stimuli for a receiver can be auditory (hearing), visual (seeing), tactile (touching), olfactory (smelling), gustatory (tasting) or any combination of these. Your gestures and touch, how you dress, comb your hair and smile all communicate to others and also to yourself. Meta-messages are messages about other messages (communication about other communication), e.g. in conversations people may say, 'Did you understand me?'; 'Was I clear?'; 'What did you say?'; 'Can you repeat what you said?'.

- Feedback messages – These are messages sent back to the speaker in order to relay the receiver's reaction to what has been said.

- Feed-forward messages – These messages are sent before sending the primary messages, e.g. the preface or table of contents in a book; the opening paragraph of a chapter; a movie preview.

- Channel – The medium through which messages pass influences the form and content of your messages, and can either enhance or create barriers (noise) to your communication. Consider for instance the differences when communicating in contexts such as at a funeral, football stadium, restaurant, market, or night club.

- Purpose – The reason for your interpersonal communication might be to learn, to relate, to influence, to play, to help.

- Ethics – Because communication has consequences, interpersonal communication also involves ethics – the moral dimension, rightness or wrongness of your communication. Since ethics are intertwined with your own culture and philosophy of life, it is difficult to state universal principles on this point.

There are many different types of relationship that can be formed in this world, but few are as important as the relationships between people who share their workspace. The way team members relate to each other in a professional environment is vitally important, because these individuals have such a significant effect on the overall quality of each other's lives. If you do not relate well to those with whom you interact on a daily basis, you might experience enormous problems that can affect not only your health and emotional well-being, but can also threaten your financial security. Following is some advice to minimise friction and assist you in understanding and relating to the people with whom you work.

- Emotional intelligence (EI) – the ability to perceive, control and evaluate emotions. Some researchers suggest that emotional intelligence can be learnt and strengthened, while others believe it is an inborn characteristic. Peter Salovey and John D. Mayer (1990) define emotional intelligence as 'the subset of social intelligence that involves the ability to monitor one's own and others' feelings and emotions, to discriminate among them and to use this information to guide one's thinking and actions'. It's about recognising your own emotional state and the emotional states of others. Emotional intelligence is also about engaging with others in ways that draw people to you. Emotional intelligence consists of four core abilities (Navigation Learning 2012):

- Self-awareness – the ability to recognise your own emotions and how they affect your thoughts and behaviour, know your strengths and weaknesses, and have self-confidence.

- Self-management – the ability to control impulsive feelings and behaviours, manage your emotions in healthy ways, take initiative, follow through on commitments, and adapt to changing circumstances.

- Social awareness – the ability to understand the emotions, needs and concerns of other people, pick up on emotional cues, feel comfortable socially, and recognise the power dynamics in a group or organisation.

- Relationship management – the ability to develop and maintain good relationships, communicate clearly, inspire and influence others, work well in a team, and manage conflict.
- Assertiveness – your willingness to stand up for your rights while respecting the rights of others. Non-assertiveness is an inability to assert oneself or stand up to defend one's rights in most or all situations (generalised non-assertiveness) or in certain situations (situational non-assertiveness). Aggressiveness is behaviour that serves self-interests without any consideration for the rights of others. Steps towards increasing your assertiveness include:
  - Analyse the assertive communications of others.
  - Analyse your own communications.
  - Rehearse assertive communications.
  - Communicate assertively.

It is important to understand how communication takes place in the workplace. Following are some characteristics of workplace communication and relationships.

Directions in which communication can flow:

- Upward communication – messages sent from the lower levels of the hierarchy to the upper levels.
- Downward communication – messages sent from the upper levels of the hierarchy to the lower levels (e.g. manager to customer service employee).
- Lateral communication – messages sent from equal to equal (e.g. manager to manager, waiter to waiter).
- Grapevine communication – messages that don't follow the formal structure of the organisation (can be sent from anyone to anyone).
- Workplace group communication – messages between members of a workplace group that has been established in order to achieve a certain outcome or complete a project.

Workplace relationships can influence work, communication and individuals. Three of these are:

- Romantic relationships – Although these can have benefits, romantic relationships at work can often cause problems that would not arise in other contexts.
- Mentoring relationships – An experienced person helps a younger or newer employee learn the ropes of the organisation.
- Networking – This enables you to expand your areas of expertise and access information that can be used to solve problems, answer questions and make decisions.

Cultural awareness means understanding that not all people are the same. Different people have different values, different behaviours, and sometimes fundamentally different approaches to life. Wherever you live and work in PNG today you will be in constant contact with people from a huge range of cultural backgrounds. In the tourism and hospitality business this is true of both co-workers and customers.

In addition, the tourism and hospitality business demands high standards of personal presentation among staff. The following five personal presentation standards are applicable across the industry, in addition to the specific standards set by any particular establishment.

1. Personal hygiene and grooming – This concerns personal cleanliness and attention to hygiene. It reflects your personal and professional image in the workplace, and should help impress customers. The following points are important:
   - Cleanliness – Bathe or shower daily and ideally after any vigorous physical activity.
   - Skin care – Both males and females should choose skin-care products that are within their price range. Clean and moisturise the skin daily.
   - Hands – Both men and women should have clean hands and nails. Women may wear clear nail polish while on duty.
   - Hair care – Hair should be clean and tidy. If your organisation allows longer hair, tie it back from your face while on duty, both for safety and hygiene.
   - Facial hair – Men should be clean-shaven or must keep their beard or moustache clean, neat and trimmed; women with facial hair problems may want to seek medical advice and treatment.
   - Dental care – Maintain your oral hygiene in order to prevent bad breath and embarrassment. Seek dental treatment if any problems arise.
   - Make-up – Natural looks are preferable, but if cosmetics are used, they should look as natural as possible.
   - Jewellery – Follow your organisation's policy.
2. Poise and deportment – Poise refers to a person's confidence and calmness. Deportment refers to the way you walk and stand, and includes your behaviour. These qualities apply to both male and female staff. The image you project should include having good posture and being pleasant, confident in the environment, customer-oriented and ready to assist. All of these make a customer's first impression a positive one.
3. Speech – Refers to your pronunciation and the clarity, tone and speed of your voice.
4. Etiquette – Refers to acceptable standards of social behaviour, particularly in regard to matters of personal address, table manners, door-opening, customer greeting and entry and departure.
5. Correct wearing and maintenance of uniforms – Look after your uniform and wear it proudly. Your uniform presents an image of you and your organisation to the customers.

There are many interpersonal skills that you can adopt immediately: take care in your appearance; face the person you are speaking to; maintain eye contact; smile and establish **rapport**; address the customer by name; listen attentively; ask questions as part of the conversation; maintain good posture; stay at a social distance (one metre apart); respond promptly to any complaint or query. The way in which you apply these skills in a particular situation should also depend on the type of customer you are dealing with and what may and may not be acceptable to them. However, these are useful as a general guide.

Describe the social and interpersonal skills desirable in a workplace where you are dealing with people from different cultures and backgrounds.

Unit 12.3 Activity 3A: Social and interpersonal skills in the workplace – short-answer questions

1. Describe what could be considered noise in the following situations:

    a. The teacher has asked you a question in class and you're trying to answer.

    b. You're doing your industry practical and the head chef is trying to explain instructions to you in the kitchen.

    c. You're having a job interview with the manager while people are working nearby.

2. What workplace social and interpersonal skills should you demonstrate under the following circumstances:

    a. Going for a job interview.

    b. Meeting a Japanese tourist.

    c. Working with a team on a project.

Unit 12.3 Activity 3B: Interpersonal skills appropriate for the setting – a case study

Following is an extract from a journal article analysing the experiences of professional women working abroad in Japan, China and Turkey (source: Napier & Taylor 2002). Read the extract and then discuss the implications of this case study for workplace social and interpersonal skills among people working in the tourism industry in PNG.

Women also agreed on the criticality of having and using interpersonal skills in settings abroad. Many commented that they tended to be good listeners anyway, to be interested in people and finding ways to interact with them positively, so adjusting to a different culture was not quite as difficult for some of them as for some of their foreign male colleagues. In fact, several mentioned that they felt women's generally more skilful interpersonal interactions were an advantage in dealing with local co-workers, subordinates and those outside the firm. Several in China, for instance, talked about the difficulty of getting good accurate information for business use. Because of that, many women said they had sharpened their listening skills and 'used' their interpersonal skills to draw out information from reluctant Chinese (especially men).

Some women admitted that they had not had strong interpersonal skills prior to working abroad, but learned from their hosts how to develop them. One senior manager in Japan, having climbed the ladder in a very male-oriented, engineering-focused firm, found herself bringing in candy, learning to remember and acknowledge people's birthdays and family members, walking visitors back to the elevator to say good bye, and generally spending more time on socializing at the beginning of meetings than she ever did in the US. She felt that using those interpersonal skills had enhanced her credibility, her ability and effectiveness as a manager of and with the Japanese.

Women also talked about learning the subtle art and skill of 'timing' and patience to gain information. Again, this issue came up most pointedly in Shanghai, where the Chinese women (from North America or Asia, with Chinese language skills) felt their understanding and use of timing and patience was better than that of foreign men, partly because of their Chinese background and partly because of their being women, which they felt gave them an advantage in getting information important for their work.

The only women we found facing difficulties regardless of their interpersonal skills were younger Japanese-American women (less than 35 years old) working in Japan. We talked to two women, both of whom found that Japanese secretaries (who were older than the women we interviewed) were apparently resentful and thus thwarted the efforts of the Japanese-American women professionals: they found their work was not done on time, had more errors than that of their male colleagues and their phone messages were ignored or recorded incorrectly. They attributed this to possible jealousy or frustration on the part of the Japanese women who did not have the same types of opportunities as the younger Japanese-American women.

Unit 12.4 Tour Guiding
Topic 1: Introduction to tour guiding

The final Unit focuses on the knowledge and skills required to work as a tour guide. Students are expected to:
- Demonstrate an understanding of the principles of good management and customer service.
- Communicate tourism information in a variety of ways and settings.

This Unit requires students to identify, describe, explain and comment on the following concepts and issues in tourism:
- Introduction to tour guiding.
- Identifying types of tour guide.
- Identifying attributes of a tour guide.
- Explaining ethics in tour guiding.
- Describing local knowledge required by guides.
- Providing a tour commentary.

We have all, at one time or another, been guided in some way, whether to help us understand a situation, gain knowledge or experience something new. Guiding has a long history in PNG. Traditionally, guiding might have involved moving one's family group from one place to another and deciding where to stay (resettlement); accompanying or giving directions to a lost traveller; inducting a clan member into survival methods such as hunting and fishing; assisting an individual's resettlement and induction into a new society as a result of marriage obligations; or parents guiding their children through land boundaries and significant cultural spots. In previous Units we learnt the importance of tourism to modern economies; it is the tour guide's job to make a tourist's experience in a destination more meaningful, enjoyable and educational.

A tour guide is not merely someone who hangs around with tourists. A tour guide should be experienced in this type of work, have in-depth local knowledge, show care and concern for tourists, offer assistance with luggage and other practical tasks, and be constantly in communication with, and visible to, the tourists under their care. A tour guide presents an image of themselves, the destination and their employing organisation. A tour guide influences whether tourists have a good experience that will lead to repeat visits and positive recommendations.

Tour escorting, in particular, has become one of the most attractive and sought-after jobs in the travel industry. Being an international tour guide is seen as a luxurious job that involves visiting exotic places, trying out different cuisine, hotels and beaches, all at the company's expense. While being a tour guide can be a fun and fulfilling job, it has its own challenges. As Goodrich points out, a good tour escort needs self-assurance, tact, diplomacy and scholarly knowledge. He or she must also have the performance skills of an entertainer, and excellent organisational and time management abilities. (Goodrich 1990).

The tourist guide's main job is to escort groups or individual visitors from abroad, or from the guide's own country or locale, around various places of interest (attractions), and offer **interpretation** services (explaining the meaning of what tourists experience). A guided tour is a sightseeing tour with a tour guide who picks the clients up from an agreed spot (this could be their accommodation or any other specified place), shows clients attractions according to an itinerary, gives explanations (interpretation) and takes the clients back to the original departure point. The services of a tour guide are usually restricted to a particular geographic area. The guide will be with a group (or individual tourist) for half a day or a full day, and will ensure that all aspects of the tour run smoothly and according to plan. The guide aims to be perceived by customers in a positive and professional way. A big part of the guide's job is to ensure that the group members are happy and having an enjoyable time.

The two main categories of tourists who may require the services of a tour guide are FITs (**fully independent travellers**), who make their own bookings based on individual interests, then might seek the assistance of a tour guide; and group travellers (who travel in a group, having bought a package tour which has been organised by others from beginning to end). The components of a package tour usually include accommodation, meals, transport, sightseeing and entertainment.

Tourists join guided (group) tours for some of the following reasons:

- A guided tour saves time and money.
- The tourist can enjoy the companionship of people with similar interests.
- The tourist doesn't need to organise or decide anything; they can just relax.
- All commentary is provided; visitors don't need to study beforehand or try to find out about a place themselves.
- Visitors are being taken care of by the tour guide.
- Tourists feel safe in the group with the guide.
- Tourists learn while travelling.

Identifying types of tour guide

To the public, the generic term 'tour guide' suggests any person who leads an organised group of people, whether for an hour to the local town market, a week along the Sepik River or a month visiting different provinces of PNG. But according to Mancini (2001), the term 'tour guide' has a precise meaning within the tourism industry: someone who takes people on sightseeing excursions and offers interpretation of limited duration. There are many kinds of tour guides:

- On-site guide or local tourist guide – conducts tours of one or several hours' duration at a specific attraction e.g. a museum, village, church, cemetery, sanctuary or waterfall; can be done on foot or in a vehicle.
- Docent – an on-site guide who works free of charge or as a volunteer, e.g. a museum volunteer who offers guiding and interpretation.
- City guide – points out and comments on the highlights of a city, usually from a motor coach, minibus or van, but sometimes as part of a walking tour. A driver-guide does double duty by narrating while driving the vehicle. A personal or private guide takes a small number of individuals on their own exclusive tour. These guides are often taxi drivers and use their taxis as sightseeing vehicles.
- Specialised guide – someone whose expertise or skills are unique, e.g. adventure guides who lead mountain climbing, trekking or diving expeditions.
- Shore excursion, ground operator (land operator or receptive operator) – large local tour companies that provide vehicles and other limited services to outside tour companies and may also employ guides.
- Step-on guide – independent or freelance specialist guide who is called upon to provide his or her services.

- National tourist guide – provides general information about the whole country.
- General tourist guide – covers many types of tours such as city sightseeing, excursions and a visit to a museum or historical monument.

Other terms used in the industry include the following:

- Tour leader – also called tour courier, director, manager or escort. This person remains with the group throughout a multi-day tour. For example if a group of US tourists does a tour in PNG, the tour leader accompanies the group from its departure in the US until its return to the US. He or she coordinates local tour guides, administers the tour, and is the contact person for the tour participants in all matters.
- Tour operator – enters into contracts with hotels, restaurants, attractions, airlines, motor coach operators and other transportation companies (or carriers) to create a multi-day tour package, which is then sold to the public directly or through travel agents.
- Inbound operator – a sub-category of tour operator, specialising mostly in groups arriving in a specific city, area or country, e.g. Trans Niugini Tours or Melanesian Tourist Services.
- Outbound operator – another sub-category of tour operator: takes groups from a given city or country to another city or country. They may use their own tour escorts or hire the services of ground operators. An example is PNG Holidays, a tour company in Australia that sends tourists to PNG.
- Motor coach and intermodal operator – creates tours of usually a week's duration that transport group members via motor coach to their destinations and back. Intermodal operators combine several forms of transportation, such as plane, motor coach, ship and rail, to create a diversified and efficient tour package.
- Incentive house – a specialised tour company or a division of a large travel agency; approaches a corporation proposing a strategy to boost sales, service or efficiency by providing some sort of reward or incentive to the corporation's most productive employees. Usually involves travel with team members to further reinforce company spirit and networking.
- Meet and greet – company that hires guides, escorts, or other 'greeters' to be on hand when individuals or small groups of travellers arrive at an airport. Greeters will help visitors get their luggage and may even accompany or drive them to their hotel (cost is paid in advance).
- Convention or meeting planner – sometimes hires tour guides and tour managers to operate pre- or post-convention tours.

There is a difference between tour conducting and tour guiding. Tour conducting is about managing tours; it involves travelling and staying with a group, controlling and entertaining people, dealing with problems and at times guiding tours. A tour conductor might remain with a group for up to two or three weeks, depending on the type of tour. Tour guiding, on the other hand, is usually for a shorter period. It refers to the specific activity at a sight or an attraction for a scheduled length of time.

A few of the pros and cons of being a tour guide:

- You get to travel to great vacation spots while getting paid for it.
- If you work hard you may get good tips, making your salary very competitive.

- Freelancing is an option, giving you maximum work schedule flexibility, although there are currently few opportunities for freelancing in PNG.
- You learn a great deal and can become the expert on a destination or itinerary. Research is one of the requirements of becoming a tour guide.
- Work is not always available – most work depends on the season.
- You must undertake thorough research about the destinations, especially if you are new to it.
- Not all clients are easy to get along with; some can be troublesome, or harsh in their criticism, especially if they are not impressed by the level of service you offer.
- The job involves mobility, stress and responsibility (although in PNG this applies mostly to bigger operators dealing with large groups).

Tour conductors and guides work for tour operators, incentive houses and many other organisations. An ideal tour manager is outgoing, decisive, organised, ethical, inquisitive and has good speaking and people skills.

Attributes of a tour guide

The informal and formal attributes of a successful tour guide include the following:

- Outgoing personality (is energetic).
- People skills (cares about people, listens to clients).
- **Diplomacy** (is tactful).
- Objectivity (can analyse and see both sides of a situation).
- Ability to find solutions to problems quickly.
- Ability to anticipate problems.
- Love of travel.
- Ethical attitude.
- Common sense.
- Sense of humour.
- Professional approach.
- Effective communication and presentation skills.
- Good personal presentation.
- Sound knowledge.
- Efficient time management.
- Ability to work in a team.
- Decisiveness.
- First-aid training.

There are many tasks and routines a tour guide may need to undertake at one time, for example:

- Completing a head count.
- Providing information on an attraction/city.
- Reconfirming scheduled appointments.
- Handling and fixing all sorts of problems.
- Liaising with other travel and tourism personnel.

Briefly described below are some personal attributes of a successful tour guide:

- Leadership skills – The tour guide must keep the group under control. He or she sets the pace; gives the group instructions on what to do; always walks ahead of the group; decides what is to be done.
- Personal presentation – Remember: You never get a second chance to make a first impression. Wear clean and neat clothes that are appropriate for the occasion, type of clients and activity to be undertaken (bushwalking: walking boots, shirt and trousers; city tour for business people: for men, shirt and dress trousers; for women, a dress and clean shoes).
- Good health and personal hygiene – Always have clean hair and fingernails; no chipped nail polish; avoid strong perfumes and too much make-up; clean teeth and fresh breath.
- Cheerful disposition – Leave your problems at home. Be lively and interesting, but always behave in a respectful and polite way. Show a sense of humour.
- Problem-solving skills – Have alternatives prepared, in case you need them. Always stay calm and don't panic. Listen to the problems and complaints of your clients first. For instance, if the town market is closed, take your group to another market outside of town. Be patient with difficult guests. Don't think of a guest as badly-behaved unless they do it three times.
- Knowledge of clients and their background – Learn about the clients' nationalities and special interests. Be open to the ways of different cultures and learn how to deal with different people. Know where the tour has already been and where it will be going later.
- In-depth knowledge of the tour – Do your research beforehand and keep up to date in your local knowledge.
- Good communication skills – Speak loudly and clearly; make lively and engaging comments and be enthusiastic about the places you show clients. This will inspire your group.

Ethics in tour guiding

A tour guide must exercise diplomacy and tact to ensure smooth and pleasant relationships with their participants. This can be achieved by following these rules of conduct:

- Remember that your behaviour contributes to the country's and company's image. You are the representative of the country and the company.
- Be tidy and well dressed.
- Be friendly and outgoing.
- Show good manners and avoid nervousness. Keep calm in all circumstances.
- Answer all questions with care and honesty.
- It is better to admit that you don't know the answer to a question than to give misleading information.
- Don't make negative judgements about other countries and their beliefs, customs or politics.
- Avoid recommending people or places of doubtful reputation.
- Don't discuss personal problems with your clients.
- Give equal attention to all clients and not only the particularly attractive or outgoing ones.
- Do not allow your conduct with clients to become over-familiar.

- Help your clients keep the places you visit clean. Provide garbage bins or bags.
- Never ask for gifts or tips.

Additional suggestions for a tour guide when running a sightseeing tour:

- Be at the meeting point well ahead of time. The tour guide should be the first to arrive.
- Greet each tourist as they arrive and invite them to take a seat on the coach or bus.
- Make sure that all tourists who have signed up for the tour are present. Do a head count.
- Once the group is assembled, give them a warm welcome.
- Introduce yourself.
- Introduce the driver.
- Give a brief rundown of the tour program, mentioning the highlights of the tour.
- If there is a microphone on the coach or bus, sit at the front looking out the window in the same direction as the driver and give a commentary as each sight appears.
- If you stop the coach for your clients to get off, make sure to tell them why you are stopping and what you will be doing there. Tell them how much time they will be spending at the site and when they should be back on the bus.
- Be sure to help older clients get on and off the bus.
- Before you leave a site, make sure that all clients are back on the bus. Do a regular head count.
- When clients get off the bus at a site don't leave them entirely unassisted. Structure the visit by giving them information first and leaving them to explore alone after that, if appropriate.
- When speaking to the group outside the coach, face them and maintain eye contact. Position your group in such a way that they can see the attraction and hear your comments.
- Never stand up while the coach is moving.
- Tourists love taking photographs. Be familiar with popular photo locations and the preferences of your clients and make photo stops if appropriate.
- Make sure your clients have access to toilets at regular intervals.

We have established that there are different kinds of tour guides and operators. But all these people should be trustworthy, energetic, patient, organised, adaptable, flexible, ethical, knowledgeable and people-oriented.

Local knowledge required by guides

A tour guide must possess a good general knowledge about PNG that includes the following topics:

History – the origins of PNG's people

- Scientists believe the first people came to New Guinea about 50 000 years ago. These people fished and hunted animals with simple tools and ate wild plants.
- About 30 000 years ago people began settling in the Highlands and on some islands.
- About 9000 years ago Highlanders began growing some foods. They were among the world's first gardeners.

History – early European contact

- Early 1500s – New Guinea is sighted by Portuguese and Spanish navigators, but remains largely isolated from the rest of the world.
- 1526 – First contact made when Jorge de Meneses docks his ship at the spot later named Port Moresby.
- 1873 – British sea captain John Moresby surveys the harbour of what would become the National Capital District. He names its two sections Fairfax Harbour and Moresby Harbour.
- 1874 – Reverend William G. Lawes establishes a headquarters of the London Missionary Society near Hanuabada.

History – European colonisation

- 1884 – Germany formally takes possession of certain northern areas later known as the Trust Territory of New Guinea. Britain establishes a protectorate over present-day Central, Gulf, Milne Bay, Oro, Southern Highlands and Western provinces, with headquarters at Port Moresby.
- 1886 – Vice-Admiral G.E. von Schleinitz becomes the first administrator of German New Guinea. British New Guinea is declared a colony, and William MacGregor begins ten years as administrator. He starts a policy of government by patrol.
- 1890 – Church leaders and MacGregor set up spheres of influence.
- 1898 – George Le Hunte begins five years as lieutenant-governor of British New Guinea.
- 1899 – German government takes over from the New Guinea Company, making Herbertshohe (Kokopo) in East New Britain its headquarters, and expanding government stations and roads.

History – Australian administration

- 1901 – Britain announces plans to transfer British New Guinea to the newly independent government of Australia.
- 1905 – Australia's parliament passes the *Papua Act*, accepting British New Guinea as a territory and naming it Papua. Overland mail begins between Port Moresby and Kokoda.
- 1906 – Australia adopts a land ordinance controlling leases of Papuan land by Europeans.
- 1907 – Hubert Murray begins 33 years as lieutenant-governor of Papua.
- 1910 – Rabaul becomes headquarters for German New Guinea.
- 1914 – German areas are occupied by Australian troops and remain under military administration.
- 1921 – Trust Territory of New Guinea becomes a League of Nations mandate administered by Australia. New Guinea is administered under the mandate and Papua under the *Papua Act*.

History – World War II

- 1939 – War breaks out in Europe.
- 1941 – Japan and USA enter the war.
- 1942 – Japan invades Papua New Guinea and civil administration is suspended.
- 1945 – Japan surrenders to the Allies.

History – Independence

- 1970 – Beginning of gradual assumption of powers by the Papua New Guinea government, culminating in formal self-government in December 1973.
- 1975 – 16 September: Papua New Guinea achieves full independence within the British Commonwealth.

Geography

- PNG is part of Oceania. It comprises more than 600 islands (including the eastern half of the island of New Guinea), located between the Coral Sea and the South Pacific Ocean, east of Indonesia.
- PNG lies 6°S and 147°E.
- PNG has a total area of 462 840 square kilometres (land 452 860 square kilometres; sea 9 980 square kilometres).
- One of the most striking features of PNG is the immense variety of its landscape. Highlands, plateaux, valleys, savannah, rainforest, mangrove swamps, gardens, plantations, islands, archipelagos and coral atolls provide a spectrum hardly matched anywhere else in the world. There are at least 100 volcanoes, some still active, and a large number of geothermal springs.
- South of the central cordillera on the main island stretch luxuriant lowlands, interlaced with one of the largest river systems in the world.

Climate

- Tropical; northwest monsoon (December to March), southeast monsoon (May to October); slight seasonal temperature variation.
- Coastal temperatures range from 23 °C to 30 °C. The Highlands are considerably cooler, occasionally falling to 0 °C.
- Most parts of the country have more than 2000 mm of rain per year. Weather patterns are becoming unpredictable due to changing global weather patterns.

Vegetation

- About 70% of the country is covered by vast rainforests. Other woodland covers 10%. However, rainforests are subject to deforestation through increasing commercial demand for tropical timber, pollution from mining projects and severe drought in some areas.
- As well as hundreds of different kinds of trees, there are over 10 000 species of flora. This great wealth and variety of vegetation are largely the result of the diversity of habitat.
- The most common habitat is lowland forest. With a canopy towering 30–40 metres high, these are made up of palms and vines, interspersed with ferns and orchids.
- At higher altitudes, mountain forests of oaks, laurels and conifers ultimately give way to low, dense scrub.

Fauna

- PNG has more than 150 species of mammal and 700 species of bird including 38 species of bird of paradise, over 300 species of parrot, lory and cockatoo, and 11 species of the renowned bowerbird.
- There are over 50 species of bat; several species of wallaby; the Raffray bandicoot, one of the largest in the world; two species of crocodile – freshwater and saltwater; 90 species of snake of which 43 are poisonous (seven are regarded as deadly, including the death adder).

- Nearly 200 species of lizard inhabit the mainland and islands, falling into four main groups: monitors, dragons, geckos and skinks.
- Among the several hundred species of spiders, only two are dangerous to humans: the huge bird-eating spider and the smaller redback spider. There are hundreds of indigenous species of moths and butterflies.

People (population)

- PNG has Melanesian, Papuan, Negrito, Micronesian and Polynesian races. While most people are Melanesians, Papua New Guineans vary widely in their physical characteristics, ethnic backgrounds and cultural types. PNG is in fact the most heterogeneous country in the world. It has over 800 different languages and cultural groups, within a population of just over seven million people. About 87% of the people live in rural areas.
- About 15% of the total population live in the ten major urban areas of PNG. Port Moresby, the capital city, has over 200 000 residents. Other urban population estimates include Lae (over 100 000), Madang (over 32 000), Mt Hagen (over 28 000), Wewak (over 27 000) and Goroka (over 20 000).
- Age structure in 2011: 0–14 years: 36.4% (male 1 145 946; female 1 106 705); 15–64 years: 60% (male 1 907 787; female 1 802 144); 65 years and over: 3.6% (male 121 207; female 103 802).
- Population growth rate: 1.936% per annum; birth rate: 25.92 births per 1000 population; life expectancy at birth: male: 64.23 years; female: 68.79 years; total population: 66.46 years (all 2012 estimates).

Arts and culture

- PNG's traditional cultures are embodied in the dress, dances, ceremonies, stories, songs, dramatic performances and magic practices of the different groups; material items; words and language; musical instruments; patterns/rituals and designs.

Religion

- Roman Catholic 27%; Protestant 69.4% (Evangelical Lutheran 19.5%, United Church 11.5%, Seventh Day Adventist 10%, Pentecostal 8.6%, Evangelical Alliance 5.2%, Anglican 3.2%, Baptist 2.5%, other Protestant 8.9%); Baha'i 0.3%; Indigenous beliefs and other 3.3% (2000 census).

Education (literacy)

- The proportion of people aged 15 and over who can read and write: 57.3%; male: 63.4%; female: 50.9% (2000 census).

Government

- PNG is a constitutional parliamentary democracy and an active member of the British Commonwealth. Queen Elizabeth II is the head of state, represented by her appointed governor-general.
- In 1972 Michael Somare became the chief minister of a democratically elected government and led the nation to self-government on 1 October 1973. PNG became an independent nation on 16 September 1975 with Michael Somare as the first prime minister.

- The national government is made up of three independent branches: the executive, the legislature and the judiciary. In 2012 PNG experienced a constitutional and political crisis in which two opposing individuals claimed to be the legitimate prime minister, each side making its own government appointments and disputing the allocation of seats in the parliament.

- There are 19 provinces and the National Capital District, each with its own provincial government. In 2011 two new provinces were created: Hela (separated from Southern Highlands Province) and Jiwaka (separated from Western Highlands Province). Provincial governments receive grants from the national government for functions such as capital works and maintenance, health, education, agriculture, town planning, forestry and business development.

Economy

- PNG's *Medium Term Development Strategy 2005–2010* focused on ten guiding principles: private-sector-led economic growth; resource mobilisation and alignment; improvements in quality of life; natural endowments; competitive advantage and the global market; integrating the three tiers of government; partnership through strategic alliances; least-developed areas intervention; empowering Papua New Guineans and improving skills; and sweat equity and Papua New Guinean character. The *Vision 2050* document identifies seven pillars of advancement: human capital development, gender, youth and people empowerment; wealth creation, natural resources and growth nodes; institutional development and service delivery; security and international relations; environmental sustainability and climate change; spiritual, cultural and community development; and strategic planning, integration and control.

- GDP real growth rate (taking into consideration inflationary pressures): 9% (2011 estimate); GDP per capita (taking into consideration remittances and income from abroad): US$2500 (K5300, 2011 estimate).

- Composition by sector: agriculture: 30.3%; industry: 37.7%; services: 32.1% (2011 estimate). Labour force: 3.896 million (2011 estimate); proportion employed in agriculture: 85% (2005 estimate); unemployment rate: 1.9% (2008 estimate).

- Budget (2011 estimate): revenue: US$4.191 billion (K8.917 billion); expenditure: US$4.151 billion (K8.832 billion); taxes and other revenues: 36.8% of GDP; inflation rate (consumer prices): 8.4%.

- Agricultural products: coffee, cocoa, copra, palm kernels, tea, sugar, rubber, sweet potatoes, fruit, vegetables, vanilla, shellfish, poultry, pork.

- Industries: copra crushing; palm oil processing; plywood production; woodchip production; mining of gold, silver and copper; crude oil production; petroleum refining; construction; tourism. Electricity production (2008 estimate): 2.965 billion kWh; consumption: 2.757 billion kWh; oil production: 30 570 barrels per day (2010) and exports: 8029 barrels per day (2009); natural gas production: 130 million cubic metres (2009) and consumption: 130 million cubic metres (2009).

- Exports: US$7.566 billion (K16.098 billion, 2011 estimates). Export commodities: oil, gold, copper ore, logs, palm oil, coffee, cocoa, crayfish, prawns. Main export partners (2010): Australia 27.9%, Japan 9.1%, China 7.1%.

- Imports: US$4.945 billion (K10.521 billion, 2011). Import commodities: machinery and transport equipment, manufactured goods, food, fuels, chemicals. Main import partners (2010): Australia 42.1%, Singapore 13.1%, China 7.9%, Japan 6.6%, USA 4.3%.
- Exchange rate: kina per US dollar: K2.12766 (March 2012).
- PNG's current economic growth has been hastened by the LNG (liquefied natural gas) and other resource developments in the country. Tax incentives by the PNG government have encouraged many domestic and foreign investments in the country, with particular growth in the telecommunications industry.

Communications

- Telephone system: generally, services are minimal. They include radio-telephone and telegraph, coastal radio, aeronautical radio and international radio communication services. Domestic access to telephone services is limited although combined fixed-line and mobile-cellular teledensity has increased to roughly 35 per 100 persons.
- International telecommunications: submarine cables to Australia and Guam; satellite earth station: 1 Intelsat (Pacific Ocean); international radio communication service (2009).
- Broadcast media: two television stations – one commercial station operating since the late 1980s and one state-run station launched in 2008; satellite and cable television services are also available; state-run National Broadcasting Corporation operates three radio networks with multiple repeaters and about 20 provincial stations; several commercial radio stations with multiple transmission points as well as several community stations; transmission of several international broadcasters (2009).
- Number of Internet users: 125 000 (2009).
- Telephone country code: +675.
- Internet country code: .pg.

Transportation

- Airports: 562 (2010); with paved runways: 21; unpaved: 541; heliports: two (2010); roadways: total 9349 kilometres, paved 3000 kilometres; unpaved 6349 kilometres (2011); ports and terminals: Kimbe, Lae, Madang, Rabaul, Wewak.
- International airlines: Air Niugini, Qantas, Airlines PNG; domestic airlines: Air Niugini, Airlines PNG, Travel Air, Islands Nationair, Trans Niugini Airways; MAF.
- Jackson's International Airport is the gateway to Papua New Guinea; it is situated about 8 kilometres from the main centre of Port Moresby.
- Longer-distance travel within PNG is mostly by air. A good network of roads connects the Northern Zone and the Highlands Regions. There are hire and rental cars, local boats and ferries, taxis in larger towns, plus local buses (known as PMV or public motor vehicles). There is no land link between the Northern Zone and Port Moresby because of the rugged terrain. There are plans to construct new roads, so in the future there may be roads connecting the Northern, Highlands and Southern Regions.

A good tour guide should also know what is on offer in other provinces – e.g. major sites, attractions and accessibility – so that you can answer tourists' queries accurately and make informed recommendations. This broader knowledge leaves a good impression on visitors and helps you better represent your organisation and your country to the world.

Providing a tour commentary

Firstly, learn the basics of good presentation. You need to interpret what the tourists are experiencing so that the experience becomes meaningful to them. Research by Professor Albert Mehrabian analysed how we assimilate information from a presentation. He concluded that 55 per cent of the information we take in is communicated visually, 38 per cent by the spoken word and only 7 per cent is communicated through reading. For an on-site tour guide, **vocal** delivery is particularly important. Presentations of this kind are also called a tour commentary, which is referred to as 'guide-speak'.

Guide-speak is a form of public speaking. All the elements of good presentation are fundamental to the job of the tour guide:

- Use short, simple, clear words.
- Use simple phrases, not convoluted meandering. Commentary should be succinct and clear.
- Focus on the topic or attraction. Be authentic and stay on track.
- Do not overlook personal appearance.

Following are ten tips to prepare for public speaking:

- Know your material.
- Practise, practise, practise.
- Know your audience. Greet some of the group members as they arrive. It's easier to speak to a group of friends than to strangers.
- Know the location. Arrive early, walk around the speaking area and practise using the microphone and any visual aids.
- Relax. Begin by addressing the audience. It buys you time and calms your nerves. Pause, smile and count to three before saying anything. (One one-thousand, two one-thousand, three one-thousand. Pause. Begin.) Transform nervous energy into enthusiasm.
- Visualise yourself giving your speech. Imagine yourself speaking, your voice loud, clear and confident. Visualise the audience clapping – it will boost your confidence.
- Realise that people want you to succeed. Audiences want you to be interesting, stimulating, informative and entertaining. They're rooting for you.
- Don't apologise for any nervousness or problem – the audience probably never noticed it.
- Concentrate on the message – not the medium. Focus your attention away from your own anxieties and concentrate on your message and your audience.
- Gain experience. Mainly, your speech should represent you – as an authority and as a person. Experience builds confidence, which is the key to effective speaking.

Unless the commentary is pre-recorded and delivered through hand-held audio devices, a good presentation is largely dependent on the qualities of the presenter. Following are some characteristics of a good presenter:

- Starts by introducing herself or himself.
- Looks and smells good.
- Is motivated.
- Speaks clearly and strongly so that everyone can hear and understand.
- Uses good language.
- Uses the hands to show and guide.

- Presents the material in a logical order.
- Maintains eye contact with the audience.
- Rehearses the presentation, but does not memorise it word-for-word.
- Is well informed.
- Is able to answer questions; gives apologies for questions he or she cannot immediately answer.
- Looks later for answers he or she was unable to provide immediately.
- Knows when to talk and when to stop.
- Is free of 'noise' in terms of appearance and the type of message being delivered; no gaudy or loud clothing; the look is professional, but distinct from the members of the touring group.

Tour commentaries are the narratives that tour guides use to describe a place or attraction and to provide information about various aspects of a country to passengers on a tour. This is the business of interpretation (guide-speak). Tour commentaries can include general information and stories about the country's attractions, events and personalities, and about the particular attraction or sight.

The process for preparing tour commentaries comprises establishing the background, needs and interests of the tour group; confirming the itinerary; accessing information about the sights to be visited; researching facts about the sights; preparing the commentary text. Following are some steps in delivering a tour commentary:

- Preparatory work before the tour: confirm the characteristics (age, geographical origin, cultural background, educational level, special interests and expectations) of the tourists. Know what your commentary is meant to cover, and what can be left out.
- Start by introducing yourself and clearly stating the purpose of the tour.
- En route to attractions, as well as at the sights, present the commentary in a conversational form, not by memorisation.
- Make your commentary interesting, relevant, simple, and delivered in a logical sequence.
- Be sensitive to the interests of the group and tailor the guide-speak (interpretation) to the group.
- Seek feedback throughout the tour to ensure that you are holding the visitors' attention.
- Respond to visitor enquiries as accurately and positively as you can. When you do not immediately have an answer, refer to field guides and other sources of information.
- Focus on what you know; be specific and express the information in terms of what the tourists can see.
- If you cannot find the answer to a visitor's request for necessary information, apologise and refer the enquiry to an alternative source of information.
- Be accommodating and flexible with members of the group, allowing for different points of view and ways of doing things.
- Allow enough time at each stop for each tourist to fully enjoy the place and gain information, including allowing some time on their own.

To ensure that the tour commentary is lively and does not bore tour participants (particularly as some participants may be repeat customers), here are some hints for keeping a tour commentary lively:

- Keep up to date with what is new on the subject, or at the sight. This will give some measure of energy to the tour guide and consequently the narration.

- Strive for continuous improvement. Review your performance for the day, take an informal poll of the visitors and make changes each time.
- Look at the sight or attraction through the eyes of the visitor. Remember most may be seeing the place for the first time. Imagine what can be improved and what may be of interest; anticipate questions so that you can have answers ready.
- As a performer, draw on the group's energy. This will help you stay fresh when delivering repeated tours. Observe visitors' reactions, feel their enthusiasm, and try to liven up those who seem bored or distracted by asking open and engaging questions.

In PNG, tour guides must understand their role in dealing with emergencies, and be able to respond appropriately. In the case of a flat tyre, the guide should politely ask participants to wait patiently while the guide makes every effort to get the problem sorted out and distract them from the delay. Perhaps the guests could wait at a nearby restaurant or café while repair work is being done. If an accident occurs, apply first aid to the injured, or if the case is serious, call the ambulance and police to have the injured transported to the nearest hospital for treatment straight away. Keep written records of these incidents in case they are needed later for insurance or legal reasons.

Your work as a tour guide should be a source of personal and professional pride. In this role you are representing yourself, your employing organisation, your community, your province and your country. Tour guiding also provides you with an occupation and income. By performing to the highest professional standards, and taking care in everything you do, you will help to develop tourism in this country and create opportunities for many other stakeholders.

List some of the points to bear in mind when providing interpretation as a tour guide.

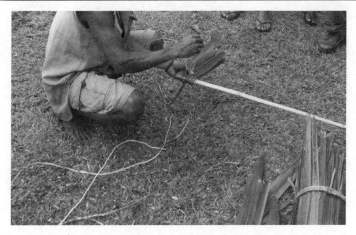

Describe the advantages of demonstration on a tour. What method might be better than a demonstration?

Unit 12.4 Activity 1A: Tour guiding – short-answer questions

1. What tasks should the tour guide do before, during and after the tour?
2. Explain the difference between a tour escort and a tour guide.
3. Describe three desirable qualities of a tour guide and three points that may spoil the performance of a guide.
4. Give reasons why tour guides are needed.
5. What do you consider are ethical issues in tour guiding?

Unit 12.4 Activity 1B: Tourist attractions in your area

Fill in the table by listing at least three tourism attractions in your area. Present your work in class.

Name or type of attraction	General description and location	Special features that make it interesting for tourists	What do guides and tourists need to bring or organise?	What could be done to develop or improve the attraction?	What could you show or point out on the way?

Answers

Unit 11.1 Introduction to the Tourism Industry
Topic 1: Tourism

Unit 11.1 Activity 1: Tourism (page 8)

1. **a.** During times of courtship in the Highlands, young men from a distant village would be invited to a traditional courtship with the young women in a local village. The men would travel to that village, where they would be welcomed and shown to the courtship house, which had been specially built for the purpose according to traditional rules. The traditional courtship would take place and eventually the men would return home after the ceremony.

    Travel such as this – to another village and then returning home – is an example of temporary travel; extending a welcome and showing hospitality to guests are tourism activities in the destination, as is the men's use of their leisure time in courtship. Therefore the young men are tourists and the activity satisfies the three elements of a tourism definition: tourists, temporary travel and involvement in tourism activities.

    b. After completing their school exams, the Grade 10 male students of Minj Secondary School in Jiwaka hire a bus to Madang. They are met by the Grade 10 male students of Tusbab Secondary School in Madang, who show them the local sites including Tusbab Beach, Machine Gun Beach, Kalibobo Lighthouse, Kranget Fish Market and Madang Town itself. In the afternoon the visitors go for a swim at Tusbab Beach. They return to the Highlands the next day.

    The Jiwaka students travelling to Madang and returning to the Highlands are undertaking temporary travel; the Highlands students being cordially received, shown around various sites in Madang and later having a swim in the sea are undertaking leisure-time activities that provide relaxation and enjoyment, which are tourism activities; the students who travelled to Madang and returned to the Highlands are tourists. This satisfies the three-concept model of tourism. (Example **a** above could also apply to this question.)

    c. After completing their school exams, the Grade 12 male students of Mt Hagen Secondary School hire a bus to Lae. On the way, they stop at Goroka, where they buy lunch from the store, which they eat while the crew refuels the bus. They then continue their journey to Lae where they are met by relatives of one of the Lae students. One of these relatives hops on the bus and guides the students on a tour of Lae City, including a visit to the Rainforest Habitat at Unitech, the Botanical Gardens and the Lae Wharf. They make a stop at Papindo Supermarket in Eriku for students wanting to do some shopping. Later in the afternoon they visit the Melanesian Hotel to try out the pizza. They depart Lae for their return journey the next day.

    In this situation, Mt Hagen is the traveller-generating region. The bus that was hired for the journey represents use of the transport sector. Goroka is the transit region; students' expenditure there represents an economic contribution by tourism to the local economy. Lae is the destination region, and the activities undertaken there by students in their free time are examples of tourism activities in the destination, while the students' expenditure in Lae represents an economic contribution by tourism to the local economy. The students' return trip shows that this trip was temporary, and therefore meets the definition of tourism. (Answer **b** above could also be expanded on for this question.)

2. **a.** Local businesses provide (for profit) the goods and services that tourists and other visitors need, such as accommodation, meals and transport.
    b. The host government helps ensure that tourists are safe; builds and maintains public infrastructure and facilities such as roads and airports; puts in place policies and guidelines to support tourism; provides incentives (such as tax breaks) to encourage investment in the tourism sector; and makes funding available to market and promote the country as a desirable tourist destination, thus helping to build a positive image.
    c. The host community owns the tourism resources; shares these resources amongst its own community members and with tourists; helps ensure that tourists are safe and have a good time; develops its resources and makes them accessible so that tourists will have quality experiences; protects these resources from damage or degradation from inappropriate tourist activities; and provides guiding and interpretation services at the destination.
    d. Publicists market and promote tourism in the area; conduct awareness programs so that host communities know what to expect of tourism; and put together tour packages which they promote to outside organisations (such as tour operators).
    e. Tourists and other visitors make tourism viable, by demanding services that are provided by other stakeholders. They spend money, which creates employment and income for workers and helps to sustain people's lives in villages. Tourists' attitudes towards conservation can help local people become aware of issues affecting the environment.

3. **a.** The marketing specialist sector.
    b. The coordinating sector.
    c. The tour operator sector.
    d. The miscellaneous sector.

4. **a.** Attractions draw tourists to the destination and become the motive for tourist travel, e.g. Nusa Island Resort and Surfing in New Ireland Province.
    b. Access to tourist sites and attractions is made possible by good roads and transport systems. Tourists need access to public facilities and complementary support infrastructure such as health-care services, communication systems, banks and post offices.
    c. Places providing overnight stays, e.g. hotels, lodges, guest houses and village stays.
    d. Additional services and facilities such as a hair and beauty salon; tea- and coffee-making facilities in a hotel room; multichannel television; wake-up calls for guests; a drop-off and pick-up service between a hotel and the airport.
    e. Village tours, swimming, canoeing, diving, mountain climbing, in-house entertainment.

Topic 2: Tourists

Unit 11.1 Activity 2: Tourists (page 13)

1. **a.** Visitor.
    b. Business travel.

    c. VFR (visiting friends and relatives).

    d. Holiday travel.

2.   1C   2E   3A   4F   5G   6H   7D   8B

Topic 3: Sustainable tourism

Unit 11.1 Activity 3A: Sustainable tourism – short-answer questions (page 22)

1.   Economic, sociocultural and environmental benefits.

2.   **a.** Tourists spend money at a local market.

    b. Tourists on a village stay interact with their hosts; they learn about each other's way of life.

    c. Tourists appreciate and take photos of a beautiful valley landscape and mountain scenery.

    d. Tourists are mesmerised watching an Indigenous dance performance; this appreciation helps to conserve this local culture.

    e. Tourists visiting a waterfall appreciate the pristine quality of the area; they avoid dropping any rubbish and the only thing they take away with them is their photographs.

3.   **a.** Tax revenue is collected from tourism (directly through visa application and departure taxes, and indirectly from businesses such as hotels and airlines).

    b. NGOs are seen as making a worthwhile contribution; this attracts funding support from various sources.

    c. Businesses profit from tourist expenditure.

    d. Host communities take pride in their cultures being appreciated by tourists; this encourages them to preserve their traditions.

    e. Visitors enjoy a unique, high-quality experience.

    f. Publicists develop a reputation for promoting activities that do not damage the environment and help local communities, thus improving their chances of gaining support.

Unit 11.1 Activity 3B: Sustainable tourism – essay (page 23)

Sample short essay:

Tugutugu Guest House is a small, family-owned and run operation on Karkar Island in Madang Province. It can be reached by a regular ferry service, which takes about three hours. There are a number of aspects of Tugutugu Guest House that make it sustainable: it was built from a combination of traditional materials found in the local environment and materials bought from the store, so it blends in visually with its surroundings; it gains aesthetic qualities from the orchid garden in front, the neat lawn and the surrounding flower trees and cocoa and coconut palms, which create an atmosphere of calmness and freshness; guests are fed with organically grown bananas and pineapples picked from the guest house's garden and with fresh fish and leafy vegetables bought locally, providing income to local fishermen, gardeners and traders; a percentage of the guest house's profits are reinvested to support community projects, so the benefits are spread across the Karkar Island community. All these factors combine to create a sustainable operation that will benefit the people and the environment today and in the future.

Unit 11.1 Activity 3C: Sustainable tourism – field report (page 23)

1.   Sample of a checklist, can add/amend. Comments to be completed after your visit.

Criteria	Comment
The project is accessible.	
It has clear signage.	
It is well developed.	
It has proper facilities and services.	
It has easy access to support facilities and services, e.g. police, aid post, telecommunications.	
There are things for visitors to do (e.g. tours, pool table) and has several attractions.	
It makes use of local resources, e.g. building design.	
It buys from locals, e.g. food.	
It provides employment for locals.	
It supports community projects.	
It has standards, rules and regulations for best practice, conservation, and use of local resources.	
Its rates are reasonable.	

Topic 4: Tourism within the local community

Unit 11.1 Activity 4: Community tourism – short-answer questions (page 28)

1. Involvement of many sectors of the community (e.g. youths, mothers, elders, workforce, students, resource/land owners, chiefs/leaders, government representatives, churches, NGOs, minority groups); better accessibility; more than one tourist attraction (many attractions); good reputation/image; educated and responsible person(s) who can provide leadership.
2. Law and order problems; a community that does not support tourism; lack of leadership and initiative to develop the concept; lack of tourism resources and/or support infrastructure; poor image/reputation.
3. Consent to tourism development on land, possibly with clear title; a benefit-sharing agreement (BSA); agreement on who will lead the decision-making process concerning the project; clear decisions on funding, construction and maintenance.

Topic 5: Impacts of tourism

Unit 11.1 Activity 5: Tourism impacts – short-answer questions (page 32)

1. Economic – Positive: employment; income; foreign exchange earnings; tax revenue. Negative: dependency syndrome (communities may come to depend on tourism to sustain their livelihood); tourism activities may take priority while other sectors of economic independence may be neglected; public funding and other resources may be diverted to tourism at the cost of other forms of development and services; inflation.

    Sociocultural – Positive: learning and education; exchanges of gifts (e.g. tourists donate funds to a local school in appreciation for the hospitality shown towards them); learning to use new technology (e.g. a tourist shows a village girl how to use a digital camera); creating better understanding of cultures on both sides; opening up people's minds and their perceptions, leading to tolerance of other people and ways of doing things. Negative: prostitution of culture (culture sold as a commodity); copycats (hosts trying to imitate tourists e.g. style of dress); foreign influence on cultures, leading to prejudices where one culture is seen as inferior to another.

Environmental – Positive: conservation measures (e.g. establishing parks); education and increased awareness of the need to protect and conserve resources to attract tourism; revenue generation from entrance fees; appreciation of resource by locals and visitors. Negative: environmental degradation from overuse and overdevelopment; natural settings being converted for tourism development; removal of important cultural resources from the environment for tourism purposes; destruction of natural habitats and ecosystems.

Unit 11.2 Tourism in Papua New Guinea
Topic 1: Introduction – Tourism in Papua New Guinea

Unit 11.2 Activity 1A: Tourism in Papua New Guinea – short-answer questions (page 39)

1. A stable government and economy and a positive rating of our government's performance by international ratings agencies (partly influenced by better world commodity prices); PNG government encouragement of foreign investment through tax incentives; developments in the telecommunications sector which boosted the country's image as a place to conduct business; further exploration and development of petroleum and mining resources – such as the LNG project – bringing more business travellers to PNG; earning foreign currencies and improving stocks of foreign reserves.
2. Culture: traditional village sing-sings, storytelling, traditional cooking (e.g. mumu and aigir). Nature: birdwatching, sightseeing, visits to zoos and parks. Adventure: trekking, mountain climbing, boating.
3. Geographical proximity (Australia is close to PNG); historical ties; PNG is a major recipient of Australian aid money and programs; Australian business and other interests in PNG.
4. The government makes available funding, the private sector upgrades all airports around the country, and citizens take on the responsibility of disposing of rubbish properly so that airports, roads and other places are kept clear of plastics and other litter.
5. Providing education and awareness is one way to develop the human capital in achieving Key Pillar 1 of *Vision 2050*.

Unit 11.2 Activity 1B: Tourism in Papua New Guinea – short essay (page 39)

Sample essay structure:
- Identify the area and its location.
- What attractive tourism features does it have?
- Make an assessment of its potential for tourism development (key factors needed for tourism development).
- Obstacles that can hinder its development.
- How the situation can be improved for tourism.

Topic 2: Tourist attractions in Papua New Guinea

Unit 11.2 Activity 2A: Tourism in Papua New Guinea – short-answer questions (page 45)

Sample answers:
1. **a.** A cave.
    b. An erupting volcano; wild animals migrating.
    c. **i.** War relics; early excavations.
      ii. Contemporary art/painting.
      iii. Farms; plantations; factories.
      iv. Resorts; scenic highways.
      v. Mega-malls; supermarkets; gift shops.
    d. **i.** PNG teams participating in international competitions, e.g. rugby and football, the South Pacific Games.
      ii. Independence Day, Queen's Birthday.
      iii. World expositions (e.g. International Tourism Bourse ITB); PNG-Made Trade Fair.
      iv. Cultural shows; music festivals; mask festival.
2. Surfing in Madang (Tupira); ecotourism in different parts of PNG; body art/painting; PNG fashion.

Unit 11.2 Activity 2B: Tourism in Papua New Guinea – field report (page 45)

Sample answer – Madang Visitors and Cultural Bureau

Principle	Comment
Resource elements	Contains specimens of cultural resources such as kundus, drums, pottery, axe heads and adzes, butterflies, old pictures, traditional bilas, musical instruments, carvings, models.
Public conceptions or understanding	The MVCB building itself is a tourist attraction based on its design and architecture; it has clear signage and is appreciated because of what it contains and the professionalism of the staff who work there.
Visitor activities	Staff will arrange tours if requested by visitors; a gift shop operates nearby.
Inviolate belt	The MVCB facility is protected by a fence and interior entrance gate; these set the building in a context and prevent unwanted visitors.
Service zone	The MVCB facility is divided as follows: the front area next to the door serves as the service zone where information and other services are provided by receptionists; situated next door (on the left just before walking through the door) is the gift shop.
Price	Very reasonable.

Summary statement – prepare your own report showing that you understand the concepts.

Topic 3: Issues – security and safety; transport

Unit 11.2 Activity 3A: Tourism in Papua New Guinea – security and safety (page 49)

1. **a.** Wear appropriate gear (e.g. proper shoes). Clear the track of any obstacles. Walk in front of the tourist and not behind. Stop regularly so that tourists can rest, catch their

breath and regain energy before continuing the walk (remember: conditions here would not be the same as in their own country).

    b. Provide protection against mosquitoes (e.g. netting over beds). Have someone visible on the premises who will look after tourists' needs. Check for any special needs (e.g. medical condition).

    c. Check how much experience the tourist has in canoeing. Check all equipment before entering the water. Carry an extra paddle. Give thought to the timing of the activity (mornings are better; if canoeing on the sea, waves may get rougher in the afternoon).

    d. Clean kitchen and cooking equipment. Use fresh ingredients. Maintain personal hygiene (for example washing hands, tying back long hair).

2. Law and order issues; community consent; accessibility (e.g. can people call the ambulance or police in an emergency?); support services (e.g. how far is the nearest aid post or hospital?); community image and reputation (e.g. have there been any bad incidents involving tourists coming to this area in the past?).

Unit 11.2 Activity 3B: Tourism in Papua New Guinea – short-answer questions (page 54)

1. Cruise ships; airlines; road and boat (via Indonesia).

2. Example (for Madang): cruise ship, airline, land, helicopter.

3. Example (for Madang): Cruise ships need to be charged a standard fee rather than different charges from different organisations. Airlines need to stick to their schedules because cancellations cost various organisations and individuals. Land transport is interrupted by potholes that become natural swimming pools after heavy rain and are impassable for humans and vehicles. Helicopter might benefit from the negotiation of better rates.

4. Example (for Madang):

Transport mode	Action	Benefit	Cost
Cruise ship	Charge a standard fee.	Convenience for cruise ships, leading to increased number of cruise calls.	Identifying which department would collect the fee and distribute the revenue among the different parties.
	Change nothing.	No-one needs to change their current structure.	Dissatisfied cruise companies, reduced number of cruise calls.
Airline	Stick to schedule.	Convenience for passengers booked on the scheduled flight; more business for suppliers such as hotels and tour operators.	Airline loses revenue if under-utilising capacity on a given route.
	Cancel flights.	Airline avoids financial losses on half-empty flights.	Dissatisfied customers; businesses lose reputation and revenue.

(continued)

Transport mode	Action	Benefit	Cost
Road	Improve and seal roads.	Lower recurrent maintenance costs in the longer term; improved local image.	Requires large up-front investment of money.
	Leave roads as they are.	No major up-front cost to those responsible, who can concentrate their resources on other areas.	Increased cost of doing business; resentment toward those responsible for roads; negative perceptions of the place.
Helicopter	Negotiate lower rates.	Improved business.	Risk of not being able to cover costs to sustain operations.
	Continue with current rates.	No additional cost pressure.	Must maintain current levels of performance or may lose existing customers; uncertainty.

Unit 11.2 Activity 3C: Tourism in Papua New Guinea – case study: Austria–PNG group tour (page 54)

1.

Day	Activity	Transport mode
1	Arrive Port Moresby (POM). Transfer to hotel. pm (afternoon) city tour.	Airline Bus Bus
2	Flight POM–MAG (Madang). Transfer and check in at hotel. Tour local market and German cemetery. Midday Kranget Island barbeque lunch and harbour cruise.	Airline Bus Bus Boat
3	Full day tour – South Coast and Balek Wildlife Sanctuary. Haya Balilna Village with sing-sing and lunch. Transfer to Gogol area; see coil pot demonstration.	Bus
4	Full day North Coast tour – St Fidelis, Alexishafen, Hole-in-the-wall, etc. Lunch and relax at Jais Aben Resort.	Bus
5	Charter MAG–HGU (Madang to Hagen) Transfer to Kumul Lodge (KL), roadside scenery. Lunch at lodge. pm tour by KL.	Airline Bus
6	After breakfast, tour of Mt Hagen city market. Lunch at KL. pm tour of local school and other interests.	Bus

Day	Activity	Transport mode
7	Full day program by KL – Waghi Valley, tea and coffee factory, villages, lunch.	Bus
8	Full day Enga Cultural Show. Dinner and overnight KL.	Bus
9	Half day Enga Cultural Show. Charter HGU–Ambunti. Check in at Ambunti Lodge.	Bus Airline
10	Full day Sepik program – nature and culture tours to Swagap and Wagu Villages. Overnight Village Guest House.	Motorised canoe
11	Full day Sepik program – nature and culture tours to Palimbe. Overnight Village Guest House.	Motorised canoe
12	Full day Sepik – back to Ambunti.	Motorised canoe
13	After breakfast, charter to WWK (Wewak). Surfside Lodge.	Airline
14	Scheduled flight WWK–POM. Ex-POM.	Airline

Unit 11.2 Activity 3D: Tourism in Papua New Guinea – transport (page 54)

Answers will vary – discuss with your teacher.

Unit 11.3 Our Neighbours and Tourism
Topic 1: Tourism and neighbouring countries

Unit 11.3 Activity 1A: Our neighbours and tourism – short-answer questions (page 60)

1. Diverse tourism products; friendly and hospitable people; some of the world's best natural and built attractions; ability to spring back after crises (such as the Asian economic crisis of 1997/98, military coups in Fiji, Bali bombings in 2002, attacks on tourists in Thailand); ability of destinations to offer bargains on travel packages for international visitors.
2. Generally safe; free from some of the world's worst problems; friendly and hospitable people; quality natural and built environments; diverse cultures.
3. Long distances; high travel costs from long-haul source markets; disease outbreaks that might be hard to control; law-and-order problems in some areas; lack of accessibility in some instances.

Unit 11.3 Activity 1B: Our neighbouring countries (page 60)

Region	Country
South Asia	Cambodia, Indonesia, Malaysia, Philippines, Singapore, Thailand, Vietnam
Oceania	Australia, Fiji, Micronesia, New Zealand, Papua New Guinea, Samoa, Tonga, Tuvalu

(continued)

Region	Country
Polynesia	Tuvalu, Tokelau, Samoa, Cook Islands, Tonga, Hawaii
Micronesia	Marshall Islands, Kiribati, Caroline Islands, Mariana Islands, Palau
North-East Asia	China, Japan, Korea, Taiwan
South-East Asia	Bangladesh, India, Iran, Nepal, Pakistan, Sri Lanka
Melanesia	Papua New Guinea, Solomon Islands, Vanuatu, Fiji, New Caledonia

Unit 11.3 Activity 1C: Our neighbouring countries – relative importance (page 61)

1.

Pacific state	Population	GDP (US$ million)	Tourist arrivals
Fiji	832 400	1 900.0	430 800
Samoa	177 700	316.0	92 300
Cook Islands	14 000	86.5	78 300
Palau	20 700	127.0	63 300
Papua New Guinea	5 520 000	4 400.0	56 200
Vanuatu	204 100	247.0	50 400
Tonga	98 300	131.0	40 100
Micronesia (FMS)	107 500	222.1	18 200
Marshall Islands	56 600	64.2	5 400
Solomon Islands	450 000	394.0	5 000
Kiribati	87 400	70.0	3 700
Niue	1 600	7.6	2 700
Tuvalu	9 600	13.0	1 500
Nauru	12 300	60.0	Less than 1 000

All three (population, GDP and tourist arrivals) would have changed since these figures were calculated. For instance, PNG's tourist arrival numbers have increased to more than 100 000 arrivals per annum; PNG's population is now over 7 million people. Other countries might experience steady growth.

2.

US$ million						
Country	1988	1989	1990	1991	1992	1993
Fiji	131	199	227	211	223	251
French Polynesia	157	138	171	150	170	164
New Caledonia	64	86	94	94	93	95

	US$ million					
Country	1988	1989	1990	1991	1992	1993
Papua New Guinea	25	40	41	41	49	45
Cook Islands	15	15	16	21	27	31
Vanuatu	11	16	22	25	30	31
Western Samoa	18	19	20	18	17	21
Tonga	7	9	9	10	9	9
Solomon Islands	5	5	4	5	12	6
Marshalls	[na]	[na]	[na]	3	3	3
Kiribati	1	1	1	1	1	1
Niue	-	-	-	-	-	-
Tuvalu	-	-	-	-	-	-
Total	434	528	605	579	634	658

Changes over 20 years will vary in each country. For example, in PNG, which is experiencing an economic boom and subsequent increase in the number of business travellers, the figures will change significantly. Other countries may be experiencing steady growth.

Topic 2: Fiji, Vanuatu and Cook Islands – case studies in tourism

Unit 11.3 Activity 2A: Tourism in Fiji – short-answer questions (page 65)

1. Government support policies and incentives for tourism development; a well-developed tourism and support infrastructure; increased marketing budgets for Fiji Visitors Bureau; increased airline capacity.
2. Military coups; overdevelopment; congestion due to tourist numbers exceeding capacity; loss of cultural authenticity.
3.

Fiji and PNG: similarities	Fiji and PNG: differences
Both countries are in Melanesia.	Fiji gets more tourists than PNG.
Both have good beaches, and friendly and hospitable people.	Fiji has a more highly developed tourism infrastructure than PNG.
Both countries were British colonies but are now independent.	PNG has more than 800 different languages and is much more linguistically diverse than Fiji.
Both countries are members of SPTO (South Pacific Tourism Organisation).	PNG has more diverse tourism products than Fiji.

Two suggested strategies: PNG governments could invest resources to improve infrastructure (such as airports, roads and bridges); ensure proper development of tourism resources before they are marketed (e.g. complying with agreed standards).

Unit 11.3 Activity 2B: Tourism in Vanuatu – short-answer questions (page 67)

1. Friendly and caring people; perceived in the market as a new tourist product; not culturally diverse, making it easier to get cooperation from its citizens to promote tourism; good resorts and beaches for water-based activities.
2. Political unrest; natural disasters; long distances from main source markets; overdevelopment; could become uninteresting if it does not diversify its tourism products.
3.

Vanuatu and PNG: similarities	Vanuatu and PNG: differences	PNG doing better than Vanuatu	PNG doing worse than Vanuatu
Both countries are in Melanesia. Both are members of SPTO. They have similar island and coastal resources. Both were British colonies, but are now independent.	PNG gets more tourists than Vanuatu (by a small margin). Vanuatu gets more cruise ships than PNG. PNG is bigger in size and population than Vanuatu. PNG has more diverse tourism products than Vanuatu.	PNG attracts more business tourists. One of PNG's hotels (Airways International Hotel) has gained international recognition. Recently PNG has invested heavily in upgrading accommodation facilities around the country (e.g. Ela Beach, Papuan Hotel, Madang Star International Hotel, Madang Resort, Gazelle International Hotel).	PNG has a reputation for law-and-order problems. Much of PNG's services infrastructure is in a poor state. PNG is a high-cost destination. Port Moresby has a negative image overseas.

Unit 11.3 Activity 2C: Tourism in Cook Islands – short-answer questions (page 70)

1. Friendly and beautiful people; tropical attractions; land- and water-based activities; well-networked islands that are easy to access; strong support from New Zealand; good air services.
2. Heavily reliant on tourism, so that anything negative could destroy the people's main industry; long distances from major source markets; threat of overdevelopment; tourists could lose interest if the country does not diversify its tourism products; natural disasters; mismanagement by authorities; emigration by its citizens could result in a lack of workforce in Cook Islands.
3. Cook Islands gains more in tourist arrivals and total tourism receipts than PNG. Tourism contributes a greater proportion (over 30%) of Cook Islands' GDP than PNG's (about 2%). Based on the latter parts of this text and the table on page 116, it can be seen that Cook Islands received more tourists than PNG (88 000 arrivals compared to 69 000), captured 0.1% of the regional market compared to PNG's 0.0%, and from 2000 to 2005 experienced an average annual growth rate of 3.9% compared to PNG's 3.6%. Based on the table on page 119, Cook Islands' total tourism receipts in 2004 were worth US$72 million (K153.2 million) compared to PNG's US$18 million (K38.3 million), as reported by UNWTO. However, this could change with PNG's current economic boom.

Unit 11.4 Tourism Information
Topic 1: Information for the tourist

Unit 11.4 Activity 1: Information for the tourist (page 75)

1.

Tourist information need	Information category
Insurance for personal valuables	Information for convenience
Universal Time Coordinates (UTC or International Time Differences)	Logistical information
Specific information concerning a restaurant: food served, opening and closing times, location	Destination/product-specific information
Tourist itinerary details	Logistical information
Information on medical treatments for malaria and cholera	Life concern information
Airline booking information	Logistical information
Description of a coastal village tour	Destination/product-specific information

2.

Information phase	Distributor	Media	Type of information
Before tourists travel	Travel agent/tour wholesaler in TGR ITO representative overseas International airline office Government mission overseas Others	Brochures, pamphlets, specialist magazines, radio, newspaper, television, shop advertisements, posters, newsletters, email/Internet, printed itineraries in TGR	Covering all four broad categories
During travel	Airlines Individuals Others	Brochures, pamphlets, magazines, audio-visuals Verbal communication	Generally covering all four broad categories, but information provided can be specific on life concern, convenience and product-specific.
When tourists are at the destination	ITO representative at airport Principal representatives Tour guides Tour escorts	Mostly printed itinerary and travel vouchers	Covering all four broad categories, providing specific information.

Topic 2: Information for the tourism industry

Unit 11.4 Activity 2: Information for the tourist industry – short-answer questions (page 81)

1. **a.** Greet customers; provide prompt service; wear clean uniforms with ID; provide clean and well-arranged facilities with adequate lighting.
   b. Clean sheets; all items in rooms neatly arranged; clean floors; proper lighting; amenities.
   c. Signage; clear tracks and paved roads; efficient arrangements; general cleanliness around the village.
   d. Mastery of the language; communicate well; professional appearance, reliable and on time.

2.

	Generic	Expected	Augmented	Potential
Ordering meat-lover pizza	Meat-lover pizza	Fast service	Sauce choice, salt and pepper	Complimentary drinks if delivery is delayed
Making a booking for a Fifth-Element hire car	Fifth-Element car	Parked at arranged spot for collection	Additional information in the car on personal protection and safety; magazine or newspaper to read	Reduced price if choice of car is not delivered
Trekking Mt Wilhelm	Mt Wilhelm	Experienced guide with good knowledge	Available equipment for rent	Free night's accommodation if climbing cannot be done (unlikely to happen!)

Topic 3: How information is delivered

Unit 11.4 Activity 3A: Delivery of tourism information (page 88)

1.

Kokopo Tours	Local tour operator (LTO) – arranges tours in East New Britain Province. It becomes an inbound tour operator (ITO) if it also brings in clients from overseas and arranges tours to other parts of PNG.
Masurina Lodge	Principal
Travel Air	Principal
Kupunung Ku Kipe Cultural Centre	Attraction
Travcoa Luxury Travel in the USA	Tour wholesaler (OTO)
PNG Holidays in Australia	Outbound tour operator or OTO

Air Niugini travel service in Australia	Travel agent
Touristik Union International (TUI) in Germany	Tour wholesaler (OTO)
Kokoda Trek	Attraction
Hertz Rent-a-Car	Principal

2. Product: One-week Madang tour package. Price: reasonably priced, based on cost of package components plus 15% markup. Promotion: through Internet social media such as Facebook. Place (distribution): through selected travel agents overseas.

Unit 11.4 Activity 3B: Analysing a case study – advertising choices (page 88)

The business wasted advertising money on media that contributed little to achieving its objectives. Most of the business was generated by existing customers, hence the business should focus on developing customer relationship programs (such as complimentary services, special rewards) to please its existing customers. This would encourage further repeat business and word-of-mouth recommendations.

Unit 12.1 Global Tourism
Topic 1: Introduction
Unit 12.1 Activity 1: World tourism – short-answer questions (page 96)

1. Definitely changed for most countries. European financial crisis causing depreciation of the Euro dollar reduces the ability of its citizens to travel abroad, particularly to long-haul destinations. The EU's (European Union) bailout plans for Greece, Spain, Portugal, Italy and Ireland, combined with strict restrictions on government spending, may cause recession in those countries. Civil unrest and uprisings in parts of Africa (e.g. Tunisia) and the Middle East (Egypt and Syria) would change tourism numbers. Recent (2012) political and constitutional crises in PNG would definitely change tourist numbers for PNG.

2. Intraregional travel would also be affected. Growth in intraregional travel in Asia is expected due to the refocus of global business towards Asia, as Europe, Africa and the Middle East face various crises. Inter-regional travel in Oceania is also expected to grow because of relatively stable and strong economic growth in Australia and New Zealand. Intraregional travel to Oceania from other zones in the Asia-Pacific region is expected to grow, as a spin-off from investment activities in Asia (in PNG, particularly LNG developments).

3. Definitely not; by looking at the tourist numbers alone, it is clear that all countries in the region do not receive equal numbers of tourist arrivals, so the level of growth would vary from country to country and also in terms of tourism impacts. There are also cost differences between countries.

Topic 2: Major geographical features of tourist regions
Unit 12.1 Activity 2: Geographical features of tourist regions – short-answer questions (page 100)

1. Boredom, ample free time and money, inconvenient weather, population pressures.

2. Convenient shops selling souvenirs, magazines, newspapers, food and toiletries; money-exchange facilities; duty-free shopping; airline agents; other principal agents (e.g. rental cars and hoteliers).

3. Political: tourists' presence improves the country's national image. Sociocultural: tourists interacting with local people leads to understanding and tolerance between different people and races. Economic: tourists' spending creates job and income opportunities in destinations. Legal: due to the threat of global terrorism, security measures are tightened around airports (e.g. passengers must pass through scanning machines). Technological: use of modern technology to make travelling more convenient for the public (e.g. e-ticketing). Demographic: tourists frequenting a particular area will also encourage citizens to move to that area in order to benefit from the opportunities created by tourism.

4.

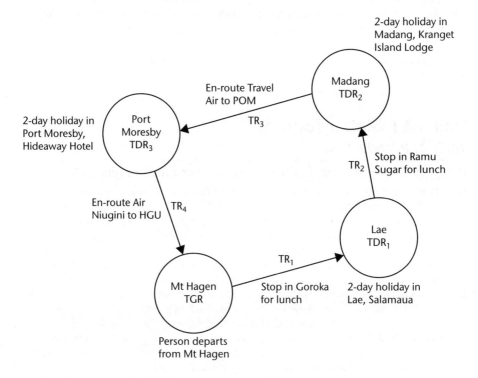

Topic 3: Characteristics of tourist regions

Unit 12.1 Activity 3A: Characteristics of tourist regions – short-answer questions (page 104)

1. Refer to the answer to Unit 12.1 Activity 2 question 4, above. Domestic tourist spending in TR_1, TDR_1, TR_2, TDR_2, TR_3, TDR_3, and TR_4 creates employment and income-earning opportunities; these organisations (principals) then pay taxes to the PNG government, which uses this revenue to deliver public goods and services to improve people's lives.

2. **a.** PNG as a tourist destination would fit into the Development stage of Butler's tourist area life cycle: PNG has recognised tourism as an industry, there are built tourism facilities and infrastructure, and PNG is attracting more tourists.

b. Example: Kalibobo Lighthouse as a tourist attraction is at the consolidation stage: it is recognised as an icon of Madang and has an established reputation as a tourist attraction for those new to Madang; although it still has appeal, further development or improvement may rejuvenate interest from both local and international visitors.

Unit 12.1 Activity 3B: Education tourism in PNG – short-answer questions (page 104)

1. Students move temporarily from where they live to where they study, and will usually return home after completion of their studies. While they are students they take part in leisure (tourism) activities such as dining in restaurants, going to pubs and nightclubs and watching sporting events. Hence their contributions have the same effects on the local environment as those of an ordinary tourist.

2.

Ordinary tourist and student: similarities	Ordinary tourist and student: differences
Both are temporary travellers.	Motives (tourism vs study).
Both engage in tourism activities.	Duration (days or a couple of weeks vs years).
Their activities have implications for destinations, principals, resources and hosts.	Expenditure (tourist may spend more in a shorter time than student).
	Tourist spend mostly within tourist industry whereas student more likely to spend in other sectors.

3. Advantages: The privileges and benefits of tourism might be extended to students. Disadvantages: Could distort statistics collected for tourism purposes, leading to false or misleading assumptions about tourism and its effects.

Unit 12.2 Tourism as a Business

Topic 1: Business sectors in the tourism industry

Unit 12.2 Activity 1: Tourism as a business – short-answer questions (page 109)

1. Accommodation sector releases hotel rooms to airline to include in its tour package, which is sold to client; client purchases the tour package, flies on the airline and stays in the accommodation.

2. **a.** Example: UNWTO. Compiles world tourism statistics and makes available destination reports.
   b. Example: PNGTPA. Also collects statistics, compiles reports and makes these available to industry members.
   c. Example: PNGTIA (PNG Travel Industry Association). Fosters coordination by initiating industry standards and best practice; markets on behalf of members; plays a representative role, e.g. in promotions overseas.
   d. Example: MVCB (Madang Visitors and Cultural Bureau). Facilitates coordination within Madang Province and markets Madang Province as a desirable tourist destination.
   e. Example: MTA (Madang Tourism Association). Provides coordination amongst its members; serves as a voice for its members; undertakes marketing activities; plays a representative role, e.g. its president attending funded training in Japan.

Topic 2: The economics of tourism

Unit 12.2 Activity 2: Tourism as a business (page 123)

1.   **a.** The total market value of final goods and services produced in the economy in any given year. It includes exports but excludes imports, intermediate goods and net income from abroad.

   b. This comprises the GDP of a country plus income from abroad, including remittances from nationals living outside and income from foreign subsidiaries of local firms.

   c. A systematic record of all economic transactions between a country and the rest of the world over a given period.

   d. Holdings of foreign currencies held by a government.

   e. Comprises internal spending on travel and tourism (total spending within a country on travel and tourism for business and leisure purposes by residents and non-residents) plus government 'individual' spending on travel and tourism services directly linked to visitors, such as cultural services (e.g. museums) or recreational services (e.g. national parks).

   f. Includes employment by hotels, travel agents, airlines and other passenger transportation services (excluding commuter services). It also includes, for example, the portion of activities of the restaurant and leisure industries directly supported by tourists.

   g. Includes wider impacts (i.e. the indirect and induced impacts) on the economy.

   h. Expenditure within a country by international tourists for both business and leisure trips, including spending on transport.

   i. Spending by government on travel and tourism services directly linked to visitors, such as cultural services (e.g. museums) or recreational services (e.g. national parks).

   j. Purchases of domestic goods and services directly by different sectors of the travel and tourism industry as inputs to their final tourism output.

2.   Discuss your answers with your teacher.

Topic 3: Business operations and employment opportunities

Unit 12.2 Activity 3A: Business operations in tourism (page 131)

A taxi driver drives recklessly, causing his passenger, a tourist, to have chest pains.	Tort
A cleaner leaves a lodge floor wet after mopping but does not put up a sign. A tourist walks on the floor and slips, injuring his ankle.	Negligence
Your mum owns and manages her own business.	Sole proprietorship
This legal entity is separate from its owners, can sue and be sued, acquire and sell real property, maintain perpetual succession, have a corporate seal, lend money, and make and alter its own bylaws.	Corporation
A tourist complains to her lawyer that her hotel had low water pressure. She wants to sue her travel agent. The lawyer advises her that she is trying to sue the wrong person.	Privity of contract
A carver is selling a carving for K25 to a local tourist. He sees a foreign tourist coming and quickly raises the price to K50.	Price discrimination

Unit 12.2 Activity 3B: Business operations in tourism – short-answer questions

1. Answers will vary – discuss with your teacher.
2. Answers will vary – discuss with your teacher.
3.

	Advantages	Disadvantages
Starting own business	Own boss Make all decisions Keep all profits Own pace of development	No proven track record of business May be difficult to get bank loan and other assistance because of no track record No existing customers
Buying existing business	Proven track record Existing customers Lower purchase price Existing employees and suppliers	Business may have bad reputation or image May take on liabilities Unsuitable location

Unit 12.2 Activity 3C: Employment opportunities in tourism – short-answer questions (page 136)

1. Low pay; long and irregular hours of work; no clear career pathway or promotion opportunities.
2. Asking for tips; enticing clients to patronise establishment, e.g. employing under-age girls to serve guests in bars and nightclubs; promotion based on gender; prostitution in some nightclubs and hotels.
3. Answers will vary – discuss with your teacher.

Unit 12.3 Customer Service

Topic 1: Introduction

Unit 12.3 Activity 1: Customer service – short-answer questions (page 139)

1. Furniture, equipment, building, people, plants, cleanliness, décor.
2. Smile, greeting, prompt and reliable service, skill or ability to offer solutions, organisational ability, mood.
3. Pre-consumption: calling to place an order for a pizza. Consumption: pizza being delivered and eaten. Post-consumption: recommending the pizza shop to friends.
4. Offer complimentary service, rewards, free gifts, free membership, discounts and other rewards and incentives.

Topic 2: Needs of various tourist groups

Unit 12.3 Activity 2: The needs of various tourist groups – short-answer questions (page 144)

1. **a.** Budget accommodation, adventurous activities, simple transportation.
   b. Binoculars, insect repellent, hat and boots, photography equipment and accessories.

    c. Solid shoes or boots, thick socks if it's cold at the summit, warm clothes, gloves, water bottle, guides.

    d. Reasonable accommodation, carriers, power source, research equipment, food rations and other supplies.

2. Wedding party: suitable location, e.g. botanical garden; professional organisation and close attention to detail; easy access to services and support facilities, e.g. airport; limousine service; romantic destination image.

Butterfly enthusiasts: butterfly farm; different species of butterflies; photographs and explanations of butterflies.

Florists and botany enthusiasts: different presentations and sources of indigenous flowers and other plants; botanical information; photographic equipment.

3.   **a.** Ensure professionalism and be time-conscious (stick to schedules; be punctual).

    b. Emphasise hygiene and respect.

    c. Focus on neatness, professionalism and courtesy.

Topic 3: Social and interpersonal skills in the workplace

Unit 12.3 Activity 3A: Social and interpersonal skills in the workplace – short-answer questions (page 149)

1.   **a.** Other students talking loudly; traffic noise from outside.

    b. Other staff banging pots and pans; distractions such as a pot boiling over.

    c. Overhearing telephone conversations of others working nearby; distraction caused by customers walking into the room.

2.   **a.** Dress neatly and professionally; research background information about the company; look and behave confidently.

    b. Be punctual, neat and professional; show respect.

    c. Understand the needs of group members; communicate well with each member; contribute to group work; show courtesy to each member.

Unit 12.3 Activity 3B: Interpersonal skills appropriate for the setting – a case study (page 150)

Women are becoming increasingly successful as professionals who can make a real contribution and compete on an equal footing with men; for this reason women and men should be given equal consideration for recruitment, training and promotion, and the opportunity to prove themselves in the workplace. This also means that a man may find himself working for a woman manager, supervisor or business proprietor; all men need to demonstrate appreciation for the contributions and ideas of women, and show respect and professional courtesy to all colleagues, regardless of gender.

Unit 12.4 Tour Guiding

Topic 1: Introduction to tour guiding

Unit 12.4 Activity 1A: Tour guiding – short-answer questions (page 167)

1. Before tour: Arrive early (before the tour participants); check out the facilities; have in your possession tour commentaries, itineraries and any other necessary information.

During tour: Make your tour commentary lively and interesting, rather than reading from a script; check to ensure everything is okay (e.g. when getting on or off the bus); stay with your group; do not let individuals wander off on their own; do a head count to confirm numbers. After tour: Ensure group is dropped off at the right location; thank the participants; seek their feedback; wish them well for the rest of their stay in PNG.

2. A tour guide takes people on sightseeing excursions and offers interpretation services for a short duration, whereas a tour escort remains with the group throughout a multi-day tour. For instance, if a group of American tourists does a tour in PNG, the tour leader remains with the group the whole time from departure in the USA until return to the USA. He or she coordinates local tour guides, administers the tour, and is the contact person for participants in all matters.

3. Desirable qualities: presentable appearance; confidence; speaks well; works well in a group context. Points that may spoil a tour guide's performance: nervousness; anxiety; lack of preparation; inadequate knowledge of the product.

4. To provide visitors with personal assurance and a sense of safety and security; to impart knowledge; to escort people and provide interpretation.

5. Asking for tips; gender issues (such as a personal relationship developing between a tour guide and a tourist); providing inaccurate information or misleading tourists.

Unit 12.4 Activity 1B: Tourist attractions in your area (page 167)

Sample answer:

Name or type of attraction	General description and location	Special features that make it interesting for tourists	What do guides and tourists need to bring or organise?	What could be done to develop or improve the attraction?	What could you show or point out on the way?
Balek Sulphur Creek and Wildlife Sanctuary	The Balek Sulphur Creek and Wildlife Sanctuary is a natural wonder of Madang. This spectacular wildlife area is situated along the Ramu Highway, 20 minutes' drive from Madang Town.	A beautiful lagoon-like sulphur creek flows out from a massive formation of limestone; fish, eels and turtles are found in the creek; surrounding tropical flowers, trees, insects and other wildlife; good picnic area with barbeque facilities.	Inform locals in advance if coming; bring photographic equipment, money for entrance fees, insect repellent, light clothing and hat.	Better signage; removing weeds and other unwanted growth; keeping tracks clear; some benches to sit and relax.	Balasiko market; four-mile market, Gum River and town water supply; Gum Primary School; junction to Bilbil.

Sources

Sources of information used in preparing this book include the following:

Abe, T. & Vincent, P. (19 September 2006). 'Growing PNG Tourism as a Sustainable Industry': Papua New Guinea Tourism Sector Review and Master Plan (2007–2017) Final Report. Port Moresby: Independent Consumer and Competition Commission & Papua New Guinea Tourism Promotion Authority.

ACTRAC Products Ltd & Australian National Training Authority (ANTA) (1996). National Generic Management Skills Level 1: Managing Operations – Customer Service Learning Guide. Melbourne: Standards and Curriculum Council of the Australian National Training Authority.

AHECS (Association of Higher Education Careers Services) & GTI Media Ltd (2012). Hospitality, Sport, Leisure and Tourism. http://gradireland.com/career-sectors/hospitality-sport-leisure-and-tourism, accessed 23 March 2012.

Airlines PNG (2006–07). Our Aircraft. www.apng.com/index.asp?pgid=84, accessed 10 March 2012.

Air Niugini (2012). Current Fleet. www.airniugini.com.pg/about-us/current-fleet/, accessed 10 March 2012.

Allen, K.R. (1999). Growing and Managing an Entrepreneurial Business. Boston: Houghton Mifflin.

Anderson, C. (2012). How to Become a Tour Guide. www.dreamtraveljobs.com/how-to-become-a-tour-guide, accessed 26 March 2012.

Atherton, C. & Atherton, T. (1998). Tourism, Travel and Hospitality Law. Sydney: LBC Information Services.

Bojanic, D. (1992). 'A Look at the Modernised Family Life Cycle and Overseas Travel'. Journal of Travel and Tourism Marketing, 1:1, 61–79.

Butler, R.W. (1980). 'The Concept of a Tourist Area Life Cycle of Evolution: Implications for Management of Resources'. In B. Boniface & C. Cooper (2005). Worldwide Destinations: The Geography of Travel and Tourism (4th edn). Oxford: Elsevier Butterworth-Heinemann.

Cateora, P.R. (1983). International Marketing (5th edn). Homewood, Ill.: R.D. Irwin.

Chieu-Freund, S. (25 May 2010). Mahonia Na Dari – Guardians of the Sea – Kimbe Bay, PNG. http://blogs.panda.org/coral_triangle/2010/05/25/mahonia-na-dari-guardians-of-the-sea-kimbe-bay-png/, accessed 2 March 2012.

CIA World Fact Book (updated 30 December 2011). Cook Islands. www.cia.gov/library/publications/the-world-factbook/geos/cw.html, accessed 13 March 2012.

—— (updated 30 December 2011). Fiji. www.cia.gov/library/publications/the-world-factbook/geos/fj.html, accessed 12 March 2012.

—— (updated 30 December 2011). Papua New Guinea. www.cia.gov/library/publications/the-world-factbook/geos/pp.html, accessed 27 March 2012.

—— (updated 30 December 2011). Vanuatu. www.cia.gov/library/publications/the-world-factbook/geos/nh.html, accessed 13 March 2012.

Collier, B. (1992). Introducing Economics (2nd edn). Brisbane: Jacaranda Press.

Commonwealth of Learning (COL) (n.d.). VUSSC Course Guide: Tour Guiding. Vancouver: COL, the Virtual University for Small States of the Commonwealth.

Cook-Islands.com.au (2012). Cook Islands Facts. www.cook-islands.com.au/facts.cfm, accessed 13 March 2012.

Crompton, J.L. (1979). 'Motivations for Pleasure Vacation'. In N. Leiper (revised 1997). *SOY00411 Tourism and Hospitality Studies I: Book of Readings*. Lismore, NSW: Southern Cross University.

Curley, Seth (7 May 2001). *'Malinowski's Kula Ring Map'*. In *Anthropology's Kula Ring: A Historiographic Introduction*. https://webspace.yale.edu/anth500/projects/01_Curley/Malinowski_Kula_Ring_Map.html, accessed April 2012.

Department of National Planning and Monitoring (March 2010). *Papua New Guinea Development Strategic Plan 2010–2030, Our Guide to Success*. Waigani: Department of National Planning and Monitoring.

de Souto, S.M. (1993). *Group Travel* (2nd edn). Albany, NY: Delmar.

DeVito, J.A. (2001). *The Interpersonal Communication Book* (9th edn). New York: Addison Wesley Longman.

Dinica, V. (2009). 'Governance for Sustainable Tourism: A Comparison of International and Dutch Visions'. *Journal of Sustainable Tourism*, 17:5, 583–603.

Douglas, N. (1996). *They Came for Savages: 100 years of Tourism in Melanesia*. Lismore, NSW: Southern Cross University Press.

Ecotourism Melanesia (n.d.). *Visit Papua New Guinea*. www.em.com.pg, accessed 2 March 2012.

eHow (1999–2012). *Sample Job Description of Hospitality and Tourism*. www.ehow.com/facts_5621997_sample-job-description-hospitality-tourism.html, accessed 23 March 2012.

Goeldner, C.R. & Brent Ritchie, J.R. (2009). *Tourism: Principles, Practices and Philosophies* (11th edn). Hoboken, NJ: John Wiley & Sons.

Goodrich, Jonathan N. (January 1990). Review of *Conducting Tours: A Practical Guide* by Mark Mancini. *Journal of Travel Research*, 29:2, 72.

Gunn, C.A. (1985). *Tourism Planning* (2nd edn). New York: Taylor & Francis. Cited in P. Pearce (1991). 'Analysing Tourist Attractions'. *Journal of Tourism Studies*, 2:1, 46–55.

Helpguide.org (n.d.). *Emotional Intelligence (EQ)*. www.helpguide.org/mental/eq5_raising_emotional_intelligence.htm, accessed 25 March 2012.

Horner, S. & Swarbrooke, J. (2004). *International Cases in Tourism Management*. Oxford: Elsevier Butterworth-Heinemann.

Imbal, J. (October 1999). *Guest Houses: Comparing Three Guest Houses in Madang Province*. Diploma Tourism Research Project 1 & 2. Madang: Divine Word University.

—— (May 2009). 'Developing the Tourism Potential of Papua New Guinea'. *Contemporary PNG Studies*, 10; 26–39.

—— (May 2010). 'Contemporary Challenges Facing the Development and Management of Culture Tourism in Papua New Guinea'. *Contemporary PNG Studies*, 12; 12–28.

International Ecotourism Society (1990–2012). *What is Ecotourism?* www.ecotourism.org/what-is-ecotourism, accessed 2 March 2012.

Jackson, I. (1989). *An Introduction to Tourism*. Melbourne: Hospitality Press.

Kandampully, J. (2002). *Services Management: The New Paradigm in Hospitality*. Sydney: Pearson Education Australia.

Kelly, I. & Nankervis, A. (2001). *Visitor Destinations*. Brisbane: John Wiley & Sons.

Kotler, P. (1997). *Marketing Management: Analysis, Planning, Implementation and Control* (9th edn). Upper Saddle River, NJ: Prentice-Hall.

Kotler, P., Bowen, J. & Makens, J. (2003). *Marketing for Hospitality and Tourism* (3rd edn). Upper Saddle River, NJ: Prentice Hall Pearson Education International.

Leiper, N. (1995, reprinted 1997). *Tourism Management*. Melbourne: RMIT Press.

Levitt, T. (January–February 1980). 'Marketing Success Through Differentiation – Of Anything'. *Harvard Business Review*, 83–91.

Malinowski, B. (1932). *Argonauts of the Western Pacific: An Account of Native Enterprise and Adventure in the Archipelagoes of Melanesian New Guinea*. London: George Routledge & Sons; New York: E.P. Dutton & Co.

Mancini, M. (2001). *Conducting Tours* (3rd edn). Albany, NY: Delmar Thomson Learning.

Mason, P. (2003). *Tourism Impacts, Planning and Management*. Oxford: Elsevier Butterworth-Heinemann.

Medlik, S. (1997). *Dictionary of Travel, Tourism and Hospitality* (2nd edn). Oxford: Butterworth-Heinemann.

Mehrabian, A. (1980). *Silent Messages: Implicit Communication of Emotions and Attitudes* (2nd edn). Belmont, CA: Wadsworth.

Milne. S. (August 2005). *The Economic Impact of Tourism in SPTO Member Countries: Final Report*. Fiji: South Pacific Tourism Organisation.

MNG00441 Tourism and Hospitality Services Management Study Guide and Readings (revised 2002). Lismore, NSW: Southern Cross University.

Morauta, R. & Arni, E. (eds.) (July–August 2000). *Welcome! Air Niugini Paradise In-flight Magazine*, 140, 64.

MTS Papua New Guinea (2011). *Melanesian Foundation*. www.mtspng.com, accessed 2 March 2012.

Murphy, P.E. (1985). *Tourism: A Community Approach*. New York: Methuen.

Napier, N.K. & Taylor, S. (2002). 'Experiences of Women Professionals Abroad: Comparisons Across Japan, China and Turkey'. *International Journal of Human Resource Management*, 13:5; 837–51.

National Strategic Plan Taskforce (November 2009). *Papua New Guinea Vision 2050: 'We will be a Smart, Wise, Fair, Healthy and Happy Society by 2050'*. Waigani: Department of Prime Minister & NEC, Government of Papua New Guinea.

Navigation Learning (2012). *Navigate Self Assessment*, http://navigationlearning.co.uk/emotion-2/.

Neuhauser, R. (n.d.). *Interpretation Skills and Tour Guiding*. Madang: Tourism and Hospitality Management Department of Divine Word University.

Open Learning Agency (1995). *Adventure Tourism Series Level III: Managing Your Operation*. Burnaby, British Columbia: Marketing Department of the Open Learning Agency.

Papua New Guinea – Australia Targeted Training Facility Tourism Promotion Authority Project (2004). *Tourism Industry Training: Customer Service Training*. Madang: Austraining International & Tourism and Hospitality Management Department of Divine Word University.

Papua New Guinea Department of Education (1987). *The Story of Our Past: Social Science Pupil Book*. Waigani: Department of Education.

—— (2008a). *Tourism Studies Teacher Guide*. Waigani: Department of Education.

—— (2008b). *Tourism Studies Upper Secondary Syllabus*. Waigani: Papua New Guinea Department of Education.

Papua New Guinea Department of National Planning and Monitoring (November 2004). *The Medium Term Development Strategy 2005–2010: Our Plan for Social and Economic Advancement*. Waigani: Department of National Planning and Monitoring.

Papua New Guinea Investment Promotion Authority (n.d.). *Favorites*. www.ipa.gov.pg, accessed 22 March 2012.

Papua New Guinea Tourism Promotion Authority (1999). *Visitor Survey Report*. Port Moresby: Papua New Guinea Tourism Promotion Authority.

—— (c. 2006). *2006 Visitor Arrivals Report*. Port Moresby: Papua New Guinea Tourism Promotion Authority.

—— (c. 2010). *August 2010 Visitor Arrivals Summary*. Port Moresby: Papua New Guinea Tourism Promotion Authority.

Pearce, P. (1991). 'Analysing Tourist Attractions'. *Journal of Tourism Studies*, 2:1; 46–55.

PNG (Papua New Guinea) Holidays (2011). *Kumul Lodge Birdwatching*. www.pngholidays.com.au/kumul-lodge-birdwatching, accessed 2 March 2012.

PRO€INVEST (c. 2004). *Tourism Sector Study in the Pacific, Executive Summary: 14 ACP Countries*. Brussels: PRO€INVEST Management Unit, Centre for the Development of Enterprise.

Rayner, V.L. (17 October 2008). *Social Skills in the Workplace*. www.skininc.com/spabusiness/management/personnel/31166099.html, accessed 24 March 2012.

Renali, C. (1991). *The Roman Catholic Church's Participation in the Ecumenical Movement in Papua New Guinea*. Rome: Pontifical University of St Thomas Aquinas (Angelicum).

Robert, R.K. (ed.) (n.d.). *Office of Tourism, Arts and Culture and the Restructuring of the Ministry of Tourism, Arts and Culture: Policy Directive*. Port Moresby: Office of the Minister.

Rowe, A., Smith, J.D. & Borein, F. (2002). *Career Award Travel and Tourism Standard Level*. Cambridge University Press.

Salovey, P. & Mayer, J. (1990). 'Emotional Intelligence'. *Imagination, Cognition, and Personality*, 9:3; 185–211.

South Pacific Tourist Organisation & Tourism Council of the South Pacific (c. 1993a). *Foreign Exchange Earnings from Tourism in SPTO Countries (in US$ million), 1988–1993*. Suva: South Pacific Tourist Organisation & Tourism Council of the South Pacific Statistical Offices.

—— (c. 1993b). *Intra and Inter Regional Tourism Flows in the SPTO Region, 1988–1993*. Suva: South Pacific Tourist Organisation & Tourism Council of the South Pacific Statistical Offices.

—— (c. 1997). *Country Analysis 1990–1997*. Suva: South Pacific Tourist Organisation & Tourism Council of the South Pacific Statistical Offices.

Starr, N. (2003). *Viewpoint: An Introduction to Travel, Tourism and Hospitality* (4th edn). Upper Saddle River, NJ: Pearson Education Prentice Hall.

Swarbrooke, J. (1995). *The Development and Management of Visitor Attractions*. Oxford: Butterworth & Heinemann.

Taga, L. & Arni, E. (eds) (2008). 'Welcome Aboard, In-flight Exercises, and Your Health In-flight'. *Air Niugini Paradise In-flight Magazine*, 2; 14, 16, 18–19.

Technical Education Division (n.d.). *Tourism and Travel Unit 5*. Waigani: PNG Department of Education.

Toastmasters International (2012), *10 Tips for Public Speaking*. www.toastmasters.org/tips.asp, accessed October 2012.

Tourism Promotion Authority Act 1993 (Independent State of Papua New Guinea)

Tourism Training Australia (2008). *Careers.* www.tourismtraining.com.au/Careers/careers.html, accessed 23 March 2012.

Um, S. & Crompton, J.L. (1990). 'A Comprehensive Overview of Choice Set Terms'. In Kelly, I. & Nankervis, T. (2001). *Visitor Destinations.* Brisbane: John Wiley & Sons.

United Nations World Tourism Organization (16 January 2012). '*Press Release: International Tourism to Reach One Billion in 2012: PR12002*'. http://media.unwto.org/en/press-release/2012-01-16/international-tourism-reach-one-billion-2012, accessed 18 March 2012.

—— (n.d.). *Sustainable Development of Tourism.* http://sdt.unwto.org/en/content/about-us-5, accessed 28 February 2012.

—— (November 2006). *Tourism Market Trends: Asia and the Pacific.* Madrid: United Nations World Tourism Organization.

—— (n.d.). *World Tourism Organization UNWTO.* www.unwto.org, accessed 21 November 2010.

Vanuatu Tourism Office (2009). *Facts on Vanuatu.* http://vanuatu.travel/vanuatu/facts/, accessed 13 March 2012.

Vincent, P. (September 2009). *Tourist Guiding Techniques.* Port Moresby: PNG Tourism Promotion Authority.

Waiko, D.J. (1993). *A Short History of PNG.* Melbourne: Oxford University Press.

Weaver, D. & Oppermann, M. (2000). *Tourism Management.* Brisbane: John Wiley & Sons.

Weaver, D.B. (2003). 'Perspectives on Sustainable Tourism in the South Pacific'. In R. Harris, T. Griffin & P. Williams (eds.). *Sustainable Tourism: A Global Perspective*, 121–37. Oxford: Elsevier Butterworth-Heinemann.

WetFeet (n.d.). *Hospitality and Tourism.* www.wetfeet.com/careers-industries/industries/hospitality-and-tourism, accessed 23 March 2012.

Wikipedia (modified 14 March 2012). *World Tourism Rankings.* http://en.wikipedia.org/wiki/World_Tourism_rankings, accessed 18 March 2012.

World Travel and Tourism Council (2012). *Travel and Tourism: Economic Impact 2012: World.* London: World Travel and Tourism Council.

—— (7 March 2012). *Travel and Tourism Forecast to Pass 100m Jobs and $2 Trillion GDP in 2012.* www.wttc.org/news-media/news-archive/2012/travel-tourism-forecast-pass-100m-jobs-and-2-trillion-gdp-2012/, accessed 18 March 2012.

Glossary/Index

accessibility (7, 102, 163): the level of ease or convenience which with something can be obtained, used or understood.

accommodation (3, 7, 35, 52, 66, 78, 86, 105, 130, 141): lodgings; facility such as a hotel, motel or guest house that regularly (or occasionally) provides overnight housing for guests.

acculturation (30, 56): changing one's culture to be more like another culture; adopting or adapting to a different culture. This happens when different cultures meet, e.g. in a school context, new students need to learn the accepted norms of behaviour.

aesthetic (15): concerned with beauty or the appreciation of beauty; e.g. tourists enjoying a traditional dance display or magnificent scenery.

alternative tourism (20): forms of tourism that seek to avoid adverse – and enhance positive – social, cultural and environmental effects; an alternative to mass tourism.

amenities (7, 10): useful services and facilities that increase the comfort and enjoyment of visitors.

ancestor (2): person related to you who lived a long time ago.

anthropologist (2): scientist who studies humankind and individual societies through their customs, beliefs and relationships.

artefact (9, 29, 42, 48, 98, 141): an object made by a person, such as a tool or a decoration, especially one that is of historical interest.

association (106–7, 127, 129): a group of people who work together as an organisation for a particular purpose. Formal associations need to follow legally approved processes to officially register their existence.

attractions (7, 30, 41–5, 68, 77–8, 86, 102, 105, 153, 165): elements of the tourist product that draw tourists to a destination or site.

attribute (56, 84, 142, 156–7): a quality or characteristic of a person, place or thing.

balance of payments (111): the difference in value between payments into and out of a country over a given period of time. Most countries aim for a positive balance of payments, meaning more money enters the country than leaves it.

bargain (35, 142–3): an agreement between parties settling what each shall give and take, or perform and receive, in a transaction or sale; something bought or sold cheaply; to negotiate over price.

boarding house (2): a facility providing accommodation and meals to residents (common in the United Kingdom and other English-speaking countries). *See also* guest house.

botanist (2): a scientist who studies plants.

business (3, 7, 15, 26, 52, 78, 101, 105–9, 125–36): trade and commercial activities; a commercial enterprise or company.

business travel (9, 33–4, 52, 64, 66, 68, 111, 113, 142): travel that is directly related to one's profession or organisation, usually paid for by one's employer; includes MICE (meetings, incentives, conferences, exhibitions).

catalyst (105–7): something that speeds up a process or brings about change.

civil (law) (129): laws covering business, contracts, estates, family relations, accidents and negligence; opposite of criminal law.

clientele (13): customers, patrons or guests who demand products and services from a supplier.

colony (2, 63, 159): a country or area controlled politically by a more powerful and often distant country.

commission (77, 83, 129, 132): payment by a supplier to an intermediary as a reward for his or her services, usually a percentage of the value of the transaction.

commodity (33, 66, 135): a product or service that can be exchanged, bought or sold, especially a raw material or agricultural crop.

communication (7, 36, 50, 71, 77, 84, 145–7, 156–7, 163): the act of exchanging information with people.

community-based tourism (20): an approach to tourism in which the needs and views of local residents are incorporated in the planning and development process.

competition (35, 53, 84, 137): rivalry between two or more organisations or individuals.

concept (1, 10, 29, 121, 153): an idea, theory, general notion or invention.

contemporary (20, 37): existing or happening now.

criminal (law) (129): law concerned with offences against individuals or members of the public; procedures for charging, trying, sentencing and punishing defendants accused of such offences; opposite of civil law.

cultural tourism (7, 16, 20): travel for the purpose of attending or participating in cultural activities such as study tours, performing arts events, festivals, visits to historic sites and monuments, pilgrimages.

culture (1, 9, 20–2, 25, 29, 52, 59, 66, 68, 72, 99, 121, 146, 157, 161): the way of life of a group of people; includes the behaviours, beliefs, values and symbols that they accept and practise at a particular time.

custom (2, 29, 66): the usual way of behaving or acting in a particular society or at a particular time; an established belief or practice.

customs (33, 48, 74, 77): special duties or taxes payable on certain imported or exported goods; the area in an airport, seaport or frontier where customs officials deal with incoming goods, baggage etc.

customer satisfaction (79, 133, 137–8): meeting or exceeding the customer's expectations in providing goods, services or experiences.

customer service (134, 137–8, 141, 147): activities undertaken by a supplier or business with the purpose of enhancing customer satisfaction.

damages (129): a sum of money awarded to a person, group or organisation (usually following a lawsuit) to compensate for a loss or injury.

demand (4, 10, 29, 41, 77, 80, 101, 104, 105, 111, 160): the quantity of a particular good or service that consumers are wanting to buy at a particular price during a specified period of time.

destination management organisation (DMO) (87): organisation in the destination responsible for policy, planning, product and quality improvement, sales, networking and marketing, e.g. PNG Tourist Promotion Association.

differentiation (137): a business strategy that aims to distinguish or set apart the organisation's products and services from those of its competitors.

diplomacy (153, 156–7): skill in dealing with people without offending or upsetting them; tact.

distribution channel (74, 85): a path along which goods and services flow in one direction (from vendor to consumer), and the payments generated by them that flow in the opposite direction (from consumer to vendor).

domestic travel (2, 113): travel within one's own country.

dynamism (132): the quality of being dynamic; being enthusiastic, energetic and active; having new ideas.

ecology (16, 19, 20, 98–9): the relationships between the air, land, water, animals and plants, usually of a particular area, or the scientific study of this.

economic (1, 9, 15–16, 25–6, 29, 56–9, 69, 91, 95, 97, 111–23, 163): of or relating to trade, industry and money; e.g. tourism-generated revenue is of economic benefit to the host community.

economy (4, 11, 33, 37, 63, 65, 77, 91, 95, 104, 111, 121, 135, 162): the system of production, industry and trade by which the wealth and resources of a country are made and used.

ecotourism (17, 21, 63, 64, 106): tourist activities with the purpose of enjoying and appreciating nature, and which promote conservation, cause little or no damage to the environment, and involve the local people.

energy efficiency (98): techniques to reduce the use of electricity, fossil fuels and other sources of energy, e.g. designing buildings to take advantage of sunlight instead of needing electric ceiling lights.

entertainment (3, 11, 41, 64, 77, 106–7, 154): plays, shows, films, television and other performances or activities that amuse or divert people.

enthusiasm (80, 84, 132, 157, 164, 166): feeling of energetic interest in a particular subject or activity and an eagerness to be involved in it.

entity (129, 131): an institution, company, corporation, partnership, government agency, university or other organisation.

entrepreneur (64, 125, 128, 135): businessperson.

environment (9, 15–20, 25–6, 29–31, 97–8, 125, 128): depending on the context, can refer to the natural surroundings, or to the general conditions, e.g. sociocultural, political, economic.

exchange rate (80, 84, 163): the value of one currency in terms of another.

excursion (2, 9, 154): a short journey (usually a day trip) made for education or pleasure.

explorer (1–2, 10): a category of travel characterised by visiting places that are largely undiscovered and not frequented by other tourists; in history, the first person from one part of the world to visit a distant part of the world (such as the first Europeans to sail to Oceania).

exports (63, 66, 69, 77, 95, 111, 113, 162): goods and services produced in one country and sold to other countries.

external or macro-environment (125): factors in the general environment that directly or indirectly influence an organisation's operations, such as political and sociocultural factors.

feminine (2): having qualities generally associated with women.

foreign exchange earnings (29, 48, 52, 57–8, 69, 111, 121): foreign currency brought into a country through activities such as tourism; countries often use these earnings to pay off their foreign debts.

fully independent travellers (FITs) (154): travellers who make their own bookings based on individual interests; they might seek the assistance of a tour guide once they are in a destination.

gateway airport (56, 163): main point of air access to a country or region, usually because of its location and other transport links, e.g. Singapore for the Asia-Pacific region; Jackson's Airport for PNG.

general sales agent (GSA) (37): a tourist operator who cannot afford to maintain an office in a particular region or country may appoint a GSA to represent it in that market through promotions, providing information to consumers and other tourism businesses and making reservations on its behalf. This important sector can bring significant income to operators. Air Niugini, for example, has GSAs in those countries deemed to be potential markets.

geography (50, 55, 97, 103, 160): the main physical features of an area; the study of the systems and processes of weather, mountains, seas, lakes, etc. and of the ways in which countries and people organise life within an area.

Grand Tour (1): a long and leisurely round trip of continental Europe, undertaken by members of the British upper classes (especially in the 18th century).

gross domestic product (GDP) (58, 111, 121): the total value of goods produced and services delivered in a country in one year. It includes exports but excludes imports, intermediate goods and net income from abroad.

gross national product (GNP) (121): GDP plus total net income from abroad (e.g. in PNG gross national product includes remittances from nationals living overseas and income from foreign subsidiaries of PNG firms).

group tour (54, 142, 154): those who travel as a group, having bought a packaged tour that is organised for them from beginning to end.

guest house (2, 4, 7, 47, 77, 85, 101, 105, 130): a small owner-managed establishment providing basic accommodation and limited service. Sometimes called a boarding house or pension in Europe.

guided tour (11, 153–4): a sightseeing tour with a guide who meets clients at an agreed place, shows them attractions according to an itinerary, gives explanations (interpretation) and takes the clients back to the original departure point.

holiday (9, 11, 33–4, 66, 68, 72, 98, 103, 134, 141): a vacation; time off work or away from home.

hospitality (2, 16, 49, 77–8, 106–7, 132, 136, 147): the art of being friendly and welcoming and offering services to guests and visitors. Can refer to food, drink, accommodation and other services that an organisation, especially an accommodation facility, provides in order to keep its guests happy.

host community (7, 15–16, 20, 26, 29): the permanent residents of a city, village or other place that receives tourists and provides for their enjoyment.

hotel (2, 7, 43, 47, 64, 66, 77–80, 105, 112, 121, 129, 132–4, 137, 142): a facility that provides accommodation, food and drink for payment, mainly to travellers and temporary residents; usually also sells meals and refreshments to other clients; often provides other facilities and services such as conference and meeting venues and catering.

hybridisation (145): combing two or more different things, resulting in something new, e.g. a local culture can change when tourists arrive, resulting in a mixture of cultures; this may lead to acculturation.

hygiene (25, 35, 133, 148, 157): the degree to which people keep themselves or their environment clean, especially to prevent disease.

immigration (35, 47, 74, 77, 102): in the tourism context, the process of checking an arriving visitor's passport and other documents so that the local authorities can determine whether they may enter the country; the place where this is done (e.g. in the arrivals area of an international airport).

imports (77, 122, 163): goods and services purchased from another country.

inbound tourism (10, 12): travel into a country from another country.

incentive (9, 21, 34, 63, 66, 77, 85, 106, 132, 155, 163): something that encourages a person or organisation to do or buy something (e.g. a discount, special offer, pay rise or government grant).

incorporation (126–9): the legal process of forming and registering a company or corporation.

indigenous (2, 25, 37, 56, 63, 77, 161): originating naturally in a place or country, rather than being introduced from another place.

Industrial Revolution (1): the period from about 1750 to about 1850, in which technological changes in agriculture, manufacturing, mining and transportation profoundly affected social, economic and cultural conditions, starting in western Europe and spreading to other parts of the world.

industry (1, 7, 33, 35, 49, 59, 77–8, 95, 129, 162): a number of firms engaged in related lines of business, using similar technologies and processes to produce similar products or services, e.g. the tourism industry; the aviation industry.

inflation (29, 112, 121, 162): a general rise in prices of goods and services.

insurance (73, 77, 128, 166): a contract (policy) in which the insurer (insurance company) agrees for a fee (premium) to compensate the insured party for loss caused by an unplanned event such as an accident, theft, damage, illness or death.

internal tourism (10): travel within a country by residents and international visitors.

interpersonal skills (145–51): the ability to communicate with other people, some of whom may have different cultures, professions, languages, gender, age or status.

interpretation (153, 165): information given to tourists about whatever they are experiencing or visiting, so that the experience becomes more interesting and meaningful to them. Relates to commentary or guide-speak.

inter-regional travel (55–7): travel between regions, e.g. travel from China to PNG involves travel from North-East Asia to Oceania.

niche market segment (64): a proportion of a larger market that has a unique set of needs or desires, such as tourists who enjoy diving or birdwatching.

nomadic travel (1): travel by nomads – communities who traditionally moved from place to place (often according to the seasons), rather than settling permanently in one place.

opportunity cost (29): the cost of an opportunity foregone as a result of choosing an alternative.

outbound tourism (10): travel out of a country.

outstation (2): a sub-station or a minor station some distance from the main station; e.g. a priest may travel to an outstation to celebrate mass and then return home to the main station.

personnel (48, 74, 156): staff, workers, employees or human resources.

place of origin or **place of residence (3, 4, 98):** where a tourist normally lives. Referred to as a TGR (traveller-generating region).

pre-industrial era (1): the time when simple tools were used in agriculture, production and commerce, before the *Industrial Revolution* (c. 1750 – c. 1850).

principals (48, 52, 83, 129): those who own and supply tourism resources and services, e.g. airline operators, hotel proprietors.

private sector (105, 106–7, 162): non-government businesses, usually having a profit motive.

public good or public service (16, 113): a good or service that is intended to benefit the general community, such as infrastructure provided by governments for public use, e.g. roads and bridges.

public place (47): a place accessible to and used by members of the general community, e.g. public beach; shopping centre; hotel.

public sector (102, 106–7, 134): the part of an economy, industry, etc. that is controlled by the government.

quality service (26, 139): service that is free from error.

quarantine (35, 48, 74): historically, isolation of a person or animal to prevent disease spreading between countries; in a tourism context today, formalities, processes and documentation for preventing spread of disease, including restrictions on importing certain foods, plants and raw materials.

rapport (148): a good understanding and ability to communicate between two people; a harmonious relationship.

recreation (1, 11, 17, 77, 102, 106–7, 121): activities that people (including tourists) do for pleasure, in their free time.

remedy (129): redress, reparation or compensation paid to a person or organisation whose legal rights have been infringed.

rescission (129): cancellation of a contract by mutual agreement. In tourism a product or service cannot be tested before it is experienced; nor can it be returned, because any defect is observed as the product is being consumed.

resource (7, 16–19, 26, 29–30, 37, 43, 56, 77, 99, 121, 162): something (e.g. land, labour, raw materials) that can be used in the production of other goods or services.

resource sector (131, 135): in PNG, the forestry, fishing, mining and agricultural industries.

revenue (29, 48, 52, 58, 78, 111, 121, 162): money coming into a business, organisation or taxation system.

safety (7, 16, 25, 47–54, 73, 128, 134, 148): the state of being safe and secure; not in danger or at risk.

seasonality (29, 31, 64, 66, 69, 134): variation according to the season or time of year; exhibits a similar pattern from year to year. Relates to activities such as agriculture, construction and tourism.

sector (7–8, 11, 35, 43, 66, 77–8, 104, 105–9, 130, 162): a part of the economy, generally comprising a number of industries (e.g. the private sector, the public sector, the tourism sector); **(in aviation: 51):** a portion of a journey by air, which may consist of one or more legs or segments. A leg is a portion of a journey between two consecutive scheduled stops on a particular flight. A segment is the portion of a journey on a particular flight from the passenger's boarding point to the disembarkation point; a segment may consist of one or more legs.

security (7, 26, 47–53, 77, 95, 103, 162): in tourism, measures taken and services provided to keep visitors safe from violence, robbery, etc.

self-contained apartment (7, 105): rented apartment with its own bathroom, cooking and laundry facilities.

selling (31, 85, 132, 142–3): the last step in the chain of commerce, where a buyer hands over money in exchange for receiving a seller's good or service; activities aimed at bringing this exchange about (e.g. advertising).

sightseeing (1, 11, 83, 153–5, 158): travel for relaxation and enjoyment, that involves looking at places, buildings, events or natural features or phenomena.

signage (25, 48, 130): placards, lights and other visual indicators that provide directions, identify places and things or give instructions or warnings.

social (1, 11, 15, 25, 29, 91, 97, 102, 121, 145–51): of or relating to society or to interactions between people, e.g. tourism enables guests and hosts to interact socially and learn from each other.

sophisticated customer (25, 74, 79, 137): customer who has travelled widely and experienced a broad range of services; may be demanding and have high expectations.

special interest group (59): in tourism, a group travelling in order to pursue a particular hobby or activity such as diving or birdwatching; more generally, a group of people who seek a particular outcome (e.g. that their industry will become more profitable) and who work together to influence political decisions to achieve this.

staff turnover (132, 134–5): staff leaving jobs in a particular organisation or industry. High staff turnover can indicate underlying problems in a company or sector.

stakeholder (8, 15–16, 26, 36, 59, 106, 166): an interested party, e.g. the destination government is a stakeholder in destination tourism activities.

stereotype (30): a fixed and widely held idea or image of a particular person, group or race, especially an idea that is unfavourable or inaccurate.

suppliers (79, 83–7, 106, 128): those who provide goods and services to tourists.

tourist product (41): what tourists purchase to satisfy their leisure needs; can include combined products and services.

traffic (2, 25, 31, 103): movement of people or goods.

transit region (4, 7, 29, 31, 98): area of activity located between the traveller-generating region and the tourist destination region, through which the tourist travels to reach their destination and when returning to their place of residence.

transportation (4, 7, 16, 29, 49–53, 77, 83, 97–8, 105, 107, 132, 163): modes of transport used in tourism.

travel agent (7, 77, 83, 86, 106, 129, 132, 155): a person or organisation selling travel services (such as transportation, accommodation and travel packages) on behalf of principals (such as carriers, hotels and tour operators) for a commission.

travel distribution process (system) (83, 85–6): the process through which travel products are distributed from principal to intermediary to final consumer and the reverse payment relationships.

traveller (1, 9, 33, 71–4, 97–8, 154–5): anyone who travels from one place to another temporarily, whether for tourism or other purposes.

travel (tour) package (7, 35, 52, 83, 85, 98, 129, 154–5): a combination of two or more elements sold as a single product for an inclusive price, in which the costs of individual product components are not separately identifiable. Also called an inclusive tour.

vacation (9, 11, 64, 137, 141, 155): holiday.

VFR (9, 34, 64, 66, 68): travel for the purpose of visiting friends and relatives.

village tourism (20): tourism in which visitors immerse themselves in the day-to-day life of a village community.

vision (19, 125): a statement that gives aspiration and direction to an organisation to help it achieve its future goals.

visiting official (2): individual delegate or member of a visiting party, representing a government or other organisation with certain powers and responsibility.

visitor (7, 9, 11, 15–16, 25–6, 33–5, 42–3, 102, 113, 142, 153, 165–6): a person travelling to a place outside their usual residence for less than 12 months, whose main purpose of visit is not for paid employment in the place visited.

visitor information centre (7, 74, 77): facility operated by a local area tourist board to assist and provide information to tourists; also markets the area as a desirable tourist destination.

vocal (164): using the voice.

Staying in a community guest house made out of traditional materials is a popular activity for visitors to PNG, who like to experience village life. The guest house can also be used for local gatherings and meetings when tourists are not staying there.

Tourists enjoy simple menus, traditional foods, and fruits and vegetables, rather than processed foods. Some visitors like to help work the garden, and collect and make traditional foods like sago and tapioca.

If you are selling traditional handcrafts to tourists, tell them where the item was made, who made it and for what purpose. Tourists like to know the story behind the item.

If a tourist is stung by a fish or insect or cuts themselves on coral, treat the wound immediately with vinegar or hot water. Coral cuts can get infected, so you should cover the cut with a plaster and use antibiotic cream.

The Crater Mountain dormant volcanic chain is part of the Crater Mountain Wildlife Management Area, known for its spectacular scenery and traditional villages.

If you operate a tourism attraction or service you should always work with your local tourism office. Keep your posters and leaflets up to date; if you change your phone number let the office know quickly; ask to be put on their website; visit regularly to tell them about your latest activities.

Learning about different cultures, traditions and ways of life is an important motivation for leisure travel.

Adventurous tourists need basic but safe accommodation after the day's exertion.

Does tourism contribute to sustainable cultural activities, or not?

The 'Asaro mud-man' of Eastern Highlands Province is well recognised outside PNG.

Activities such as kayaking and canoeing combine adventure with getting close to nature.

Natural features such as limestone cliffs jutting out of the water attract tourists to PNG.

In the tropical climate of PNG, water-based activities are a real attraction for visitors.

Papua New Guinea was the location of some crucial conflicts in World War II. Many tourists from Australia and our other neighbours are interested in military history and will visit places such as the Kokopo War Museum in East New Britain Province.

You might own the best tourism operation in PNG, but if tourists and agents can't find out about it your business will fail. Travel fairs and exchanges are essential for getting your message out to the market.

The cruise ship Amadea *contains two royal suites, 40 suites and 254 cabins.*

These headdresses combine symbols of Christianity and Indigenous traditions.

The first travel agencies were established in the 19th century. How do you think the increasing use of online services – such as passengers booking their own flights – might affect this sector of the tourism industry?

This signage is an example of regional and national cooperation in providing infrastructure.

How effective do you think is the tourism promotion slogan 'A million different journeys'?

Whether you are a tour guide, business operator or hotel employee, you should familiarise yourself with the local security and emergency services. You never know when you or a visitor may need their help.